EastEnders

20 YEARS IN ALBERT SQUARE

NO PARKING
DISCOUNT TYRES

EastEnders

20 YEARS IN ALBERT SQUARE

by Rupert Smith

TED SMART

This book is published to celebrate 20 years of *EastEnders* on BBC1.

Published by BBC Books, BBC Worldwide Ltd, Woodlands, 80 Wood Lane, London W12 0TT

This edition produced for The Book People Ltd, Hall Wood Avenue, Haydock, St Helens, WA11 9 UL

First published 2005
Text by Rupert Smith

ISBN 0 563 52269 0

Commissioning Editors: Emma Shackleton and Vivien Bowler
Project Editors: Helena Caldon, Sarah Emsley and Dee O'Reilly
Designer: Bobby Birchall, DW Design, London
Picture Researcher: Miriam Hyman
Art Director: Pene Parker
Production Controller: Arlene Alexander

Set in Helvetica Neue

Colour separations by (tbc)
Printed and bound in (tbc)

Acknowledgements:
The author and BBC Worldwide would like to thank the entire cast and crew of *EastEnders* who have been enormously helpful in the production of this book. Special gratitude is due to Mal Young, Louise Berridge, Carolyn Weinstein and Jackie Lee.

Huge thanks also goes to *Radio Times* for very generously allowing BBC Books access to its resources and material.

THE QUEEN VICTORI
Dole

Contents

The first time I went out to the lot at Elstree, and I saw how much money they'd spent building Albert Square, I realised *EastEnders* wasn't going to be something that was only around for five minutes. We knew that the BBC had big plans for the show; from the very beginning, we'd been told to keep it completely hush-hush, and you don't get that kind of secrecy surrounding any old production. Of course there were rumours flying around the business, and people were asking each other what they knew – but if anyone asked me, I just said I'd been offered a very nice job and that was all there was to it.

The original cast started working six months before the show went on screen, and our priority at that time was to get to know each other as families. We didn't want to go on cold, looking like a bunch of actors, so we spent hours in the green room sussing each other out, understanding the sense of humour and the personality behind the character. And that's what makes *EastEnders* work: these are real characters that people genuinely care about. They go through experiences that every family goes through, and they react the way real people react. When the show started out, it was meant to be very realistic, practically a fly-on-the-wall look at London lives – and that's been the backbone of *EastEnders* for 20 years now. When it strays too far from family life in ordinary homes, it can lose its way – and those of us who have been there since the start feel a great sense of guardianship over the show, and will always try to keep it true to its roots.

I've always listened carefully to what the public says, because that's the best barometer of whether or not we're doing a good job. Taxi drivers in particular will always give you an honest opinion. At first they said the show wasn't realistic, the East End wasn't like that – and then, as time went by, that changed to: 'Oh, my missus really likes *EastEnders.*' That's when we knew we were doing something right. Stories in the show have touched so many people's lives; I get letters from a lot of kids saying, 'You're just like my mum,' which pleases me. Once I got a letter from a young lad in prison, who said that seeing Pauline react to Martin's troubles made him realise how much suffering he'd put his own mother through. The power of the show, and the reason it's lasted for so long, is in those true-to-life moments.

Twenty years have passed, and I'm still playing Pauline Fowler, which I would never have believed when Julia Smith first asked me about the job back in the 80s. It's constant hard work, and sometimes I look back at pictures of myself when the show first started and there were a lot fewer lines and bags… but I'm very grateful to Pauline: she's paid for some nice holidays, a nice home, and she even got me an MBE in 2000 for services to television drama.

Wendy Richard MBE

The brains behind the Square – Julia Smith

How the Show was Born

In February 1983, two years before *EastEnders* hit the screen, the show was nothing more than a vague idea in the mind of a handful of BBC executives, who decided that what BBC1 needed was a popular, bi-weekly drama series that would attract the kind of mass audiences ITV was getting with *Coronation Street*. Over the next 24 months, progress towards this goal was made so fitfully, and with such agonising delays punctuated by periods of frenetic activity, that's it's amazing the show got off the ground at all, let alone proved strong enough to sustain 20 years of drama.

There was anxiety at first that the viewing public would not accept a new soap set in the south of England.

The first people to whom David Reid, then head of series and serials, turned were Julia Smith and Tony Holland, a well-established producer/script editor team who had first worked together on *Z Cars* and had gone on to the BBC's long-running hospital drama, *Angels*.

The outline that Reid presented was vague: two episodes a week, 52 weeks a year, and that was about it. Smith and Holland went away scratching their heads. Why did the BBC want to fill the already-full schedules with a new soap (although 'soap' at the time was not a word you heard in BBC corridors)? And how could they possibly find a story that would occupy so many hours of screen time?

The answer to the first question was simple: the BBC was prepared to clear space in the schedules by axeing *Angels* and a few underperforming dramas like *Triangle*. The answer to the second, however, was more elusive. Two ideas were proposed to Smith and Holland – a drama set in a shopping arcade, and a drama set in a mobile home park – and both, mercifully, were rejected out of hand. And that was very nearly the end of that. David Reid was replaced as head of serials by Jonathan Powell who, at first, seemed reluctant to discuss his predecessor's ideas.

Smith and Holland were prepared to concentrate on their existing projects – neither of them was exactly lacking in work as they were producing *District Nurse* for the BBC – when Powell summoned them to Television Centre and announced not only that he was backing the idea of the bi-weekly serial, but that he was also keen to create something set in contemporary London. During the conversation that followed, the words 'East End' and 'Victorian square' were mentioned – and *EastEnders* as we know it finally stirred into life.

There was anxiety at first that the viewing public would not accept a new soap set in the south of England; the received wisdom was that only shows set north of Luton had a real chance of success. Research was duly undertaken to disprove this fact, while the creative team plunged into the East End to discover what the area was really like in the early 80s. Smith and Holland were both Londoners – Holland was from a big East End family – but when they researched Victoria Square (an area suggested by Jonathan Powell) they found massive changes in areas that they thought they knew well. Instead of street markets, local pubs and close-knit cockney communities, they discovered stripped pine, Laura Ashley curtains and wine bars. However, delving further into the East End, they found what they had been searching for. In some areas there still existed a real East End spirit – an inward-looking quality, a distrust of strangers and authority figures, a sense of territory and community that Holland and Smith summed up as 'Hurt one of us and you hurt us all'.

Suitably inspired, they decided to think about putting some ideas down on paper, only to learn that, if they were to have any chance of a commission, Jonathan Powell needed a format within less than an hour for a meeting at which he was to pitch the show to his BBC bosses. And so Smith and Holland, like many a harried BBC employee before them, repaired to Albertine's Wine Bar on Wood Lane, a few hundred yards up the road from Television Centre, where, in just 40 minutes, they composed and typed up a format that was whisked over to Powell.

It was the best 40 minutes' work they ever did. The basic building blocks of the still-nameless show were put in place: a serial about 'multi-cultural, larger-than-life characters' in a run-down Victorian square, a 'fiercely territorial, incestuous almost' attitude to family and environment, a strong reliance on 'gossip, intrigue and scandal'. They even mentioned the pub, the café, the two-storey houses and the tail-end of a street market. As yet there were no characters, no storylines – but that hastily typed bit of paper did the trick, and Powell was able to give the go-ahead.

That was in February 1984, just under a year after the first meeting with David Reid, just over a year

Tony Holland, who created the show with Julia Smith

before *EastEnders* would first be shown. The target launch date was January 1985, when BBC1 was planning a major revamp of its early-evening schedules, with the new bi-weekly (as it was still referred to, never 'soap') following Terry Wogan's new chat show. That gave Julia Smith and Tony Holland just 11 months in which to write, cast and shoot the whole thing. In February 1984, however, they didn't even have a title, let alone a cast, scripts or a place to film. The project had any number of working titles – *Square Dance*, *Round the Square*, *Round the Houses*, *London Pride*, *East 8*. It was the latter that stuck (E8 is the Hackney postcode) in the early months of the creative process.

But where was this spanking new show going to be filmed? Clearly there wasn't room in Television Centre, and to film in any of the BBC's regional centres would have divorced the show too far from its London milieu. Then it was announced that the BBC had bought the old ATV Studios at Elstree in Hertfordshire, once a thriving film studio, more recently home to *Emergency Ward 10*, *General Hospital* and *The Muppet Show*. It was sadly run down – but it did provide the studio space and, with a bit of sprucing up, the facilities that were needed for the massive turnaround the new show would require. But could it ever be ready in time for a January launch?

They had 14 days in which to create 23 characters and enough storylines to sustain the show through its first months.

The original idea was to film interiors at Elstree, and to do everything else on location in a real East End square. Julia Smith and Tony Holland set out with newly appointed production designer Keith Harris to scout Hackney and its environs for something suitable. Fassett Square, just off Dalston Lane, was the nearest thing they found to a perfect location – but it had a huge old hospital dominating one side, and was in far too busy an area ever to provide a safe, controllable filming environment. The search carried on fruitlessly throughout the early months of 1984 until, finally, the decision was taken to build a brand new East End square on the back lot at

Elstree itself. The advantages were obvious: no travelling time for cast and crew, no intrusive crowds or traffic noise. But there was one big disadvantage. The Elstree lot was a scrappy, rubbish-strewn wasteland that had last been used to film *Auf Wiedersehen, Pet*. It was dirty and dingy and utterly uninspiring. Undeterred, Julia Smith picked up a stick and sketched out a preliminary plan of the Square on the sandy floor of the vacant lot. And the rest is history. Financial objections were overcome, Keith Harris and his team stormed into action and a brand-new Victorian square began to rise in the unlikely setting of a Hertfordshire rubbish dump.

Smith and Holland had everything now except a show, a script and a cast. And so, desperate to escape the incessant phonecalls and meetings that dogged their lives in London, they decamped to Lanzarote for two weeks in March 1984 armed with a portable typewriter and a case full of A4 paper. They had 14 days in which to create 23 characters and enough storylines to sustain the show through its first months before they were obliged to present something to Jonathan Powell and his colleagues at the BBC.

Their 'office' was an apartment at Playa los Pocillos near a busy tourist resort. Undistracted by sunshine, they set about creating the characters first – because the characters were to be the driving force of the storylines, rather than vice versa. Holland, who had first-hand knowledge of East End family life, was assigned the task of dreaming up the central family group, while Smith sketched out the rest – the single people, the newcomers, the outsiders.

Tony Holland started at the top, with the matriarch of the family that he'd always known would dominate the show. He drew directly on his own background: his mother, Ethel Thirkettle, was the youngest of four daughters from Walthamstow. Her oldest sister, Lou, married one Albert Beale and had two children, Peter and Pauline. Doris and Sis married two brothers, Bert and Bill Mears. Ethel married John Holland.

And so Lou Beale – the fictional one, not Tony Holland's aunt – was born. His character notes, written during that fortnight in Lanzarote, described her as an 'archetypal East End mother figure. Fat, funny, sometimes loud, often openly sentimental. An obsessive view of family…she can be a stubborn, cruel "old bag" when she wants to be…' And so it went on. Characters flowed from Holland's pen: Pauline Fowler ('conventional, salt of the earth') and her unemployed husband Arthur, their children Mark and Michelle, Pete Beale and his sexy young wife Kathy, their son Ian… They all had a history (Pete's disastrous early marriage, Kathy's hard childhood, Pauline and Arthur's humdrum marriage) and enough baggage to keep the show going for months.

Lou Beale – the Square's first matriarch

Smith and Holland created a cross-section of the East End: the old, traditional cockney culture and the new, ethnically mixed population.

Wendy Richard who, luckily for the show, was 'tired of glamour'

Smith, meanwhile, had drawn on memories of East End characters to create Ethel Skinner ('as a youngster, Ethel would have been a page three girl'), Dr Legg, Mary Smith (the single mother-punk-prostitute), the Jeffreys, the Osmans, the Carpenters… When Smith and Holland compared notes, they realised that they'd created a cross-section of the East End that they'd witnessed on those fruitless research trips around Hackney – an accurate reflection of the old, traditional cockney culture and the new, ethnically mixed population. The icing on the cake was the Watts family who ran the local pub – again, drawn directly from Holland's own experience working in London boozers. Jack and Pearl Watts and their daughter Tracey (as they were originally called) brought flash, trash and melodrama to the square; from the word go, the relationship between Mr and Mrs Watts was fraught with sexual and emotional tension.

With those precious character sketches in the bag, and with enough potential storylines to sustain the first 20 episodes, Smith and Holland returned to London for a meeting with the BBC. And, for once, everyone was in agreement. *East 8* was to be tough, violent on occasion, funny and sharp – 'set uncompromisingly in Thatcher's Britain' – and it would start with a bang. 'A size ten boot kicks down a door', behind which old Reg Cox lies dying…

The next few months saw a flurry of activity that had been all too absent up till now. Smith and Holland were free to engage a team of writers, the set was growing rapidly on the lot, and a composer and designer had been commissioned to create the title sequence. Simon May (music) and Alan Jeapes (visuals) had worked with Tony Holland on an earlier drama, *Cold Warrior* – and what they, along with fellow composer Leslie Osborne, came up with for the new show remains one of the strongest title clips in TV history. May's theme tune was being whistled all over the lot within hours of being played, while Jeapes came up with the bird's-eye view of the Thames that became the show's strongest visual symbol.

The title, however, remained elusive. *East 8* clearly wouldn't do; for one thing, all the casting agents they'd approached thought they were talking about a show called *Estate*. For another thing, they'd located the action in a fictional London borough of Walford (a cross between Holland's home turf, Walthamstow, and Stratford) with its own fictional postcode, E20. Something new was needed – and the answer was right under their noses. For months, Smith and Holland had been phoning up theatrical and literary agents asking, 'Have you got any real East Enders on your books?' One day in August 1984, Julia Smith came screaming out of her office; she'd had the eureka moment. Any doubt as to the suitability of the title (some thought it 'looked ugly written down' and was 'hard to say') were dispelled when the design decision was taken to include the central, capital 'E'. Alan Jeapes got to work, and the title was complete. But there was one big piece of the jigsaw missing.

There were no actors. Since Smith and Holland's creative brainstorming, the cast had grown from its original 23 with the addition of one crucial figure – Nick Cotton. None of the original characters, they felt, was wicked enough to have killed Reg Cox, and the writers demanded a figure that would sustain a murder mystery that clearly dominated the show from the very first seconds.

The first firm piece of casting was Bill Treacher, another *Z Cars* veteran whom Smith and Holland had had in mind from the word go in the role of Arthur. Anna Wing was another early choice – she had the face, the voice and the attitude that Tony Holland had imagined for Lou Beale. After that, casting came thick and fast. Peter Dean practically did a cockney stand-up routine in his audition for Pete Beale. Gillian Taylforth was considered too young and too pretty for the part of Kathy, until they heard her voice – as rough and gritty as a market trader's. Susan Tully, already a star from *Grange Hill*, clinched the role of Michelle with her excitement over the character's teen pregnancy storyline.

After that, things got harder. Matthew Robinson had Wendy Richard in mind for Pauline, but when he took her to meet Julia Smith she arrived looking like a movie star, far too glamorous for Albert Square. And she was already a household name from *Are You Being Served?* – would she unbalance a cast of relative unknowns? 'I'm sick of glamour,' she told Holland, 'I want to play my age.' Finally it was her enthusiasm for the show that clinched it. After her first meeting with director Matthew Robinson, she told him, 'It sounds like the bollocks, darling.'

Leslie Grantham originally auditioned for the role of Pete Beale, and impressed the directors with his deft twiddling of brown paper bags – but they felt he was far too strong and sexy to play a market trader, and cast him instead as the landlord of the

Queen Vic, Den (as he was now called) Watts. Everyone knew he was perfect for the part, but there was one little hitch: as a young man, in the army in Germany, Grantham had been convicted of the murder of a taxi driver, and served a long spell in prison. There were immediate fears that adverse publicity could damage the show – but Julia Smith stood by her decision, announced that Grantham had paid the price for his crime and that she was determined to keep him in the show, whatever the consequences.

Julia (centre) and the show's designer, Keith Harris, look at wallpaper for the Queen Vic

Where the magic happens: a script meeting with Julia and Tony

Anticipation and rumour grew in equal measure until the first transmission at 7pm on 19 February 1985.

The casting of Angie, his wife, was even harder. At first the role went to an actress called Jean Fennell, but, as rehearsals began, it became clear that she wasn't right for the role as Holland had conceived it. It fell to Julia Smith to give Fennell the bad news – and there were only four days before shooting began in which to find a replacement. Anita Dobson read with Leslie Grantham, and alternately 'spat like a tigress and purred like a kitten'. The job was hers.

And so, finally, filming was under way. Mercifully, the production was granted an extra month in which to prepare for its first night; the Wogan show wasn't ready, and the BBC1 relaunch was delayed till February 1985. The press were invited to Elstree in October to meet the cast and see the lot – and stories immediately started circulating about the show, about a rivalry with ITV (who were launching their own market-based soap, *Albion Market*) and about the private lives of the cast. Anticipation and rumour grew in equal measure until the first transmission at 7pm on 19 February 1985. Holland and Smith couldn't watch; they went, instead, back to Albertine's Wine Bar on Wood Lane, the place

EastEnders storylines became a staple of the nation's daily reading. Den's secret 'mistress', they told us, was really a man; Den would come out as gay, or get Aids, or both; Mary would drown her baby; Nick Cotton would be murdered; Arthur would murder three children and commit suicide…

But the real story, of 20 years of accelerating production, of characters' highs and lows, of controversial storylines and off-screen scandals, had only just begun.

Julia and Keith pore over plans to expand the Square

Some of the cast from the early days of EastEnders

where it all began. They received lukewarm congratulations from colleagues when the show was over, and went home to bed, feeling a bit deflated.

The next day, the viewing figures were confirmed at 17 million. The reviews were largely favourable, and viewing figures remained high. Press coverage, already intense, went into overdrive. Within weeks, the headline they had all dreaded had appeared – EASTENDERS STAR IS A KILLER – setting the tone for relations between Walford and the press for the next 20 years. By Christmas of 1985, the papers couldn't get enough of the show. 'Exclusives' about

20 years in Albert Square

How well do you know *EastEnders*? Where were you when Vicki was conceived, when Eddie was murdered, or when Phil was shot? Join us on a helter-skelter ride through 20 years of storylines, of unplanned births, short-lived marriages and suspicious deaths as we recall the plots that kept the TV nation talking. Marvel at the actors' changing hairstyles! Gasp as you remember long-forgotten scandals! And relive classic screen moments in our shot-by-shot analysis of *EastEnders*' finest hours.

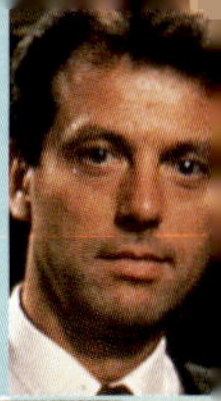

The Fowlers

When *EastEnders* began on 19 February 1985, there was no doubt in anyone's mind as to who the stars of the show were. The Fowler family were the essence of cockney kinship, a big, close-knit family with a long history, complete with a dominant matriarch in the shape of stubborn, opinionated Lou. As the year went on, Lou's position as Queen Bee in the Beale-Fowler families – and thus in Albert Square – was challenged by not one but two unexpected pregnancies from within her own family.

Pauline, the eternally downtrodden daughter, started the ball rolling when she announced, in the very first episode, that she was expecting a baby after a gap of 15 years since the birth of her daughter, Michelle. Lou was horrified at first, but despite all her bluster she was secretly pleased – this would be another little Fowler to boss around – and was easily won over by a cheap holiday in Clacton with Michelle.

But that was just the beginning of the Fowler family's problems. By the summer, it wasn't just Pauline who was pregnant and struggling to make ends meet; the increasingly depressed and irritable Michelle revealed that she too was expecting a child, although she refused to name the father. Despite intense speculation throughout Albert Square, and some heavy sessions with her father in his shed at the allotments, Michelle stuck to her guns, ignored her family's wishes (they were all for an abortion) and decided to keep the baby and finish school.

Gossip about Michelle's pregnancy quickly became a game that any number could play, and seldom were two or more Walfordians gathered together in the latter part of 1985 when talk did not turn to the identity of the mystery father. They had to keep guessing for a long time – but we knew that it was none other than Den Watts, the father of Michelle's best friend Sharon, to whom she had turned for a little bit of paternal sympathy during a difficult time over the summer, and from whom she

The Square's first family – the Fowler-Beale clan. From left to right, top: Michelle (Susan Tully), Mark (David Scarboro), Ian (Adam Woodyatt). Bottom: Arthur (Bill Treacher), Pauline (Wendy Richard), Lou (Anna Wing), Kathy (Gillian Taylforth) and Pete (Peter Dean)

got a little more than she'd bargained for. Den agreed to support Michelle and the baby, and to keep his paternity a deep, dark secret – after all, he had troubles of his own.

Despite it all, Michelle was a beacon of purity compared with Pauline and Arthur's firstborn Mark, who started out as a semi-criminal sidekick of Nick Cotton's, constantly involved in dodgy deals and even dodgier politics. On the day Nick was arrested for the murder of Reg Cox, Mark fled Walford – did he know more than was good for him? Or could he simply not stand another day under the same roof as bossy Lou, feckless Arthur, nagging Pauline and whingeing Michelle? Whatever his reasons, Mark lay low until finally contacting his family through a runaways' agency. The end of the year saw Pauline and Arthur racing down to Southend in pursuit of their long-lost son and heir who was by then working on a go-cart track and living with an older woman called Ingrid.

Lou, who began the year as the undisputed boss of the family, ended it as a shadow of her former self. Rapidly deteriorating health made her more dependent on her children than she liked, and, during Pauline's pregnancy, she was obliged to move in with her son Pete and his wife Kathy. Less able to rule the roost than she once was, Lou exercised power in the only way she knew how – by causing trouble.

Despite it all, there was one piece of good news for the beleaguered Fowlers: on 30 July Pauline gave birth to a son, Martin Albert.

Supervillain Nick Cotton (John Altman)

Nick Cotton

Walford has had its fair share of villains over the years, but none has ever measured up to Nick Cotton in terms of sheer nastiness. He was the most audacious creation of the show's original writers – a racist, homophobic bully who would stoop to any depths to make a dishonest buck, or simply to get one over on his neighbours. From the word go everyone disliked him, and with good reason: he was leading gullible youngsters like Lofty and Mark astray, involving them in right-wing politics and trying to get them into drug dealing, and he even mugged silly old Ethel Skinner, which is about as low as it gets. Ethel fought back and kneed her assailant in the groin, but spent the rest of the year quaking in fear.

Nick's minor offences were as nothing, however, compared with the murder of Reg Cox, a friendless old boy who was found dying at the very start of the first episode of 1985. Rumours and suspicions about Reg's death gradually focused and the finger of guilt began to point at Nick Cotton after a thorough and tenacious police investigation. Nick, feeling the noose tightening around his neck, fled Albert Square but was picked up in Dover and charged with a whole range of crimes, from murder down.

To the horror of his neighbours, however, Nick got off on grounds of insufficient evidence, and was back in the Square by the autumn, pretending to be a reformed character. It was a sham, of course: within moments he'd attempted to put Punk Mary on the streets, had burgled the laundry and, worst of all, started blackmailing Kathy. He'd found out, by dint of breaking into the doctor's surgery and stealing her confidential file, that Kathy had had a baby at the age of 14 – and she was willing to pay for his silence. Eventually Kathy confided in Pete, and a committee of Walford hardmen (with Den at its head) put the frighteners on Nick Cotton and drove him out of town – for the time being.

The Watts

There was never a dull moment at the Queen Victoria public house, where landlords Den and Angie Watts established themselves as the Square's answer to Richard Burton and Elizabeth Taylor. She couldn't stand the fact that he was having an affair with a posh mistress, Jan – and after a while he

The Watts family: Sharon (Letitia Dean), Den (Leslie Grantham) and Angie (Anita Dobson) in a rare moment of peace

couldn't even be bothered to cover his tracks. Heedless of Angie's suffering, Den took to disappearing for whole nights at a time, and then went on holiday to Spain with Jan, leaving poor Angie with no option but to hit the bottle and flirt with any man unfortunate enough to cross her path. Lofty, Wicksy and even Arthur felt the full force of Angie's crazed charms, but it was poor Tony Carpenter who ended up getting burnt after a brief affair that he took all too seriously.

Every so often Den and Angie tried to get their marriage back on track, if only for the sake of their adopted daughter Sharon, upon whom the constant dramas were taking their toll. Den bought Angie a microwave oven and even sent her to a health farm to dry out – but before long he was back on the phone to Jan, and his wife was back on the gin.

Ali and Sue

Ali Osman and his wife Sue started life as a rather unremarkable couple from whom nobody expected great things. He had an unfortunate penchant for gambling, frittering away the profits from the Bridge Street café and installing his brother Mehmet for all-night poker games, but that was about it – until, out of the blue, Sue and Ali found themselves at the centre of *EastEnders*' first big controversial storyline.

EVERYONE TALKED ABOUT...

It started with a kick . . .

Anyone who thought that *EastEnders* was going to be a cheerful tale of cheeky cockney folk was in for a rude surprise when, on 19 February 1985, the show opened as it meant to go on – with a death. A boot kicked open a door, and there, dying in a chair, was a lonely old man, Reg Cox. A spookily young Den Watts led the rescue posse, ably assisted by Arthur and Ali – and with friends like these, Reg never stood a chance. And so began the first of Walford's many whodunnits (and, as usual, the answer was 'Nick Cotton').

Bash! With one mighty blow of his foot, Den kicks down the door, while the cockney cavalry hovers supportively behind him

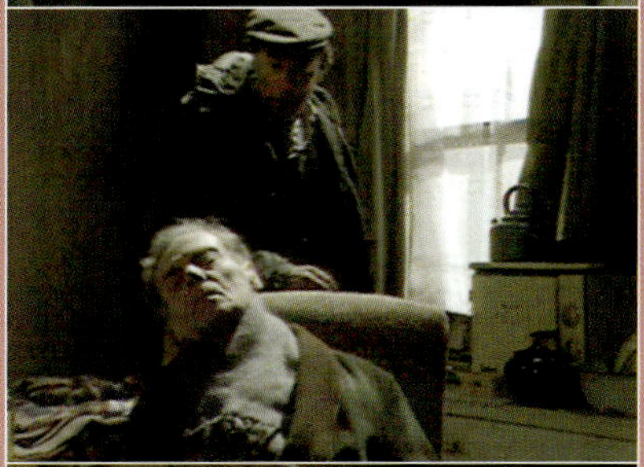

The eagle eye of Arthur Fowler notices that Reg isn't looking too well. Could that explain the odd smell?

Blimey! He's drunk a whole bottle of whisky! There's only one thing for it...

Call Dr Legg! Walford's medicine man attends the first of many casualties. On the bright side, there will soon be a vacant flat on the Square

One night in June, their baby Hassan died for no apparent reason. Sue, stunned by grief and unable to cry, moved in with Debbie and Andy, leaving Ali confused, lonely and hurt. In the wake of the tragedy, their marriage disintegrated in a welter of depression and grief until, one day, Dr Legg took the desperate measure of putting Punk Mary's baby Annie in Sue's lap, allowing her, finally, to get in touch with her pent-up sadness. Sue and Ali patched up their differences and tried to move on in life, but things could never be the same for them after the death of Hassan.

The Youngsters

Sharon and Michelle were supposed to be best friends, but they spent most of the show's first year fighting over Kelvin Carpenter. The unlikely heart-breaker wasn't terribly interested in either of them; he had problems of his own, thanks to his parents' divorce. After a few too many showdowns in the laundrette, Kelvin decided that neither of the girls was really his cup of tea, and settled down to concentrate on his exams.

Ian was more than ready to comfort Sharon, and thought his luck was in when he got a contract to do pub grub at the Vic – but Sharon didn't want to know, leaving Ian to nurse his wounded pride and pour his energies into a doomed knitwear company that he'd set up with Lofty and Kelvin. Michelle, meanwhile, got all pally with Lofty, a handy ally for a lone teenage mother-to-be, leading to the widespread assumption that Lofty must be the father of her unborn child.

The cat really got among the pigeons towards the end of the year with the arrival of another young Walfordian, Simon Wicks – Pete Beale's son by his first marriage – who instantly grabbed a job at the Vic and set about breaking every female heart in sight.

Punk Mary

Mary Smith was the Square's social conscience, an unmarried, illiterate mother of one who moved into the room vacated by the freshly murdered Reg Cox and proceeded to make every mistake she possibly could. She was exploited by sweatshops, arrested for shoplifting, got into trouble with social services for leaving little Annie 'home alone', and nearly got lured into prostitution by Nick Cotton. She ended the year on an upbeat note – for her at any rate – by getting a job as a stripper, which earned her enough money to pay for Annie's child care.

Mary Smith (Linda Davidson) with Annie

Also...

▶ Andy and Debbie campaign against plans to demolish one side of Albert Square… ▶ Michelle pretends she has a boyfriend called Carlo… ▶ Ian gets bullied for his interest in cooking, and takes up boxing… ▶ Saeed and Naima's marriage crumbles when it's revealed that he's visited a prostitute… ▶ Angie organises a ladies' darts team and gets male strippers and drag queens in to the Vic… ▶ Ethel's adored pug, Little Willy, suffers from constipation… ▶ Ian, Sharon and Michelle 'accidentally' rent a porn video…

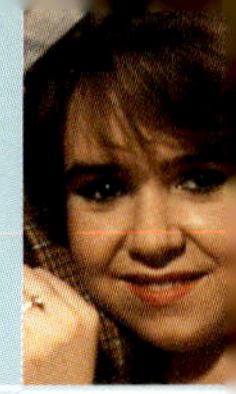

Angie and Den

The biggest story of the year, and the one that not only gripped a mass audience but also confirmed *EastEnders* as a series with serious dramatic potential, was the ugly, protracted disintegration of Angie and Den's marriage. The year started with the warring Watts trying to make a go of things, if only for Sharon's sake – but, behind the bar-room smiles, both were up to their old tricks. Den was still seeing Jan, while Angie herself was still hitting the bottle and flirting with anything in trousers in a desperate attempt to get attention.

The first crisis of the year came in March, when Angie took an overdose of sleeping pills washed down with gin, and was discovered only by accident when Den returned to the Queen Vic after a row with Jan. What started out as a cry for help almost turned into the real thing – and it didn't do poor Sharon much good when she found out that her mum was prepared to leave her in that way.

Jan (Jane How) with Den

Angie bounced back, pleased to have secured Den's attention for a little while, and set off on holiday to Ibiza full of hopes for a second honeymoon. Her dreams were dashed, however, when Den left her in the lurch and returned to London for some undisturbed nookie with Jan. Angie came back to the Square determined to salvage what was left of her pride – which she did by starting an affair with the nice male nurse Andy, temporarily estranged from Debs.

After this, things went from bad to worse. Den was increasingly distant and hostile; his mind, after all, was elsewhere, as unknown to everyone he'd just become a father for the first time in his life. Angie drowned her sorrows in a sea of booze, prompting Dr Legg to warn her that she was becoming a fully-fledged alcoholic. Faced with the truth, she broke down in front of her shrink and confessed that she was nothing but a 'clown', and that Den could never love her.

Jan, meanwhile, was losing her patience, and decided to bring matters to a head by giving Den a two-week ultimatum: leave Angie, or lose me forever. Angie knew what was coming, and used every trick in the book to avoid the confrontation – but, finally cornered by Den, she turned the tables on her philandering husband by telling him that she had a fatal illness and only six months to live. Den, revealing a rare shred of decency, realised that he could not leave a dying woman, and told Jan it was all over (it wasn't).

The reunited couple flew to Venice for a romantic holiday – which was ruined when, for reasons best known to the scriptwriters, they ran into Jan herself. Angie hit the bottle again, and in a drunken moment on the homecoming Orient Express she confessed to the barman that she'd told Den a rather large lie. And Den heard it all...

The resultant endgame lives in soap history as one of the greatest domestic dramas ever filmed. Den consulted a lawyer, and started hinting darkly about a special Christmas surprise. Angie, blithely unaware that her secret was out, went into a frenzy of festive preparations – only to be handed the divorce papers on Christmas Day itself.

Lofty and Michelle

While Den and Angie's marriage was falling to pieces, Michelle and Lofty became man and wife – but only just. A warm friendship developed into something more serious when Lofty, a chivalrous soul, decided that he wanted to take care of Michelle and her child, and proposed marriage to her. Michelle didn't say yes, but she didn't say no

Will they, won't they? Lofty (Tom Watt) and Michelle

either; being a sensible girl, she knew it wouldn't hurt to have a man in reserve when the time came.

Worried about her financial future, and overwhelmed at the responsibility of raising a child on her own, Michelle quickly decided that Lofty wasn't such a bad bet after all, even though she loved only one man – Den. Lofty had no idea, and was walking on air for a few weeks, eagerly looking for work in order to become the Great Provider. Only his chronic asthma prevented him from becoming a traffic warden.

Michelle gave birth in May to a daughter, Vicki (she later claimed that her daughter was not named after the pub on the floor of which she was conceived). Lofty smothered mother and daughter in over-eager affection, and rushed Michelle into naming the day, while the rest of the Fowler clan pressurised her into going for a big, traditional wedding with a white dress, bridesmaids (Sharon, of course) and a big reception afterwards. Michelle, stunned by childbirth, was too tired to argue (much).

On the morning of the wedding, however, she heard the still, small voice of common sense whispering in her ear, and after a tense confrontation with Den, whom she still loved desperately, she realised that she couldn't go through with a wedding that would, after all, be a sham. Lofty, left at the altar, reacted by having huge asthma attacks and repeatedly listening to Wicksy's soppy ballad 'Every Loser Wins' – could things really be that bad?

After causing maximum pain and embarrassment to everyone, Michelle changed her mind again and sneaked off with Lofty for a quick, quiet wedding away from the gaze of Walford. And so, for a while, they were Mr and Mrs Holloway.

Sharon and The Banned

Sharon Watts started to show signs of the diva-like behaviour that would make her one of Walford's most enduring female characters. Bruised by her parents' marital difficulties – and who wouldn't be? – she sought the approbation of her peers, and was a natural choice for Miss Walford 1986 when the locals staged a carnival. Sharon's pride was somewhat dented when her ceremonial throne collapsed during a test run – sabotaged, or just not strong enough for her ample figure? Undeterred, however, Sharon succumbed to the showbiz bug, possibly as a result of befriending a worldly-wise drag queen who had been briefly entertaining at the Vic earlier in the year.

Her next attempt at fame and fortune came when the Albert Square youth formed a band – with Sharon, naturally, as the lead singer and frontwoman. This not only gave her a chance to show off; it also enabled her to play off her various male admirers, among them Ian – who, for a brief but glorious time, enjoyed the romantic attentions of the girl he'd admired for so long. At first the band was called Dog Market, and, to nobody's surprise, they failed to set the world alight. After a change of image, they became The Banned – but, after one disastrous gig at the Vic, they realised that they were still useless and decided to call it a day. Sharon paraded around the Square telling anyone who'd listen that it was time to grow up and face their new responsibilities as school-leavers and job-seekers.

Arthur's Breakdown

Arthur Fowler started life as the epitome of cockney decency: a good bloke who would never set the world on fire but could always be trusted to do the right thing. That went badly pear-shaped in 1986 when, ashamed by his failure to hold down a job and desperate to give his daughter a wedding that

Arthur: happiest on his allotment

the family could be proud of, he started to dip his fingers into the Christmas Club money.

It started innocently enough. Arthur had been collecting money round the Square, and couldn't resist 'borrowing' a little to blow on an all-night poker game in the café. It soon became apparent, however, that he'd done much more than that and, when Pauline quizzed him over his lavish plans for Michelle's wedding, he confessed that he'd stolen the lot. They tried to keep things quiet, but the lies started piling up and eventually Arthur, in a moment of madness, staged a fake burglary at 45 Albert Square and told the police that all the Christmas Club money had gone.

It took the police no time at all to realise that this was an inside job, and Arthur cracked under the pressure of their interrogation. For the last few months of the year, we watched Arthur's queasy descent into depression and madness. He spent whole days doing jigsaw puzzles, watching daytime TV or locked in his shed at the allotment. Finally, on Christmas Day, he went completely crazy and smashed up the sitting room. Christmas 1986 wasn't a happy time for anyone in Albert Square.

Bad penny Pat Wicks (Pam St Clement)

Pat's Arrival

Out of the mists of time – and there were plenty who would have preferred her to stay there – came Pat Wicks, formerly Pat Beale, Pete's first wife and the mother of their son, Simon, who had also turned up on the Square in 1985 to start his career as a crooning heartbreaker.

If ever a Walford woman had a past, it was Pat. It was implied that she'd had some sort of affair with Den, and she was currently married to a man called Brian who knocked her about a bit, prompting her to return to her home patch and cause trouble there. Lou reminded her that Pete wasn't Simon's father after all; just to make matters even more complicated, it turned out that Lou thought Simon was the product of an affair with Pete's brother Kenny, so she sent him off to New Zealand.

Before you could say 'trollop', Pat had installed herself behind the bar at the Queen Vic and was embarrassing her son by wearing unsuitably low-cut tops for a woman of her age. She started casting her net far and wide, almost landing James Willmott-Brown and even making a play for the disgusting Charlie Cotton. She ended the year teetering on the brink of prostitution – a profession to which she seemed to be no stranger. Easily persuaded by Mehmet, who revealed himself as a sleazy pimp, she also dragged Mary into the gutter with her.

Debs and Andy

Debbie Wilkins was one of those Walford characters that it was impossible to care much about. She bossed around her boyfriend, nice nurse Andy, and when he got fed up with her she started dating local copper Roy Quick. When she realised that Andy was much in demand with other women in the Square (particularly Mary and Angie), Debs dumped Quick and got her man back. All seemed to be going well, and they had even started planning the wedding when Andy was knocked down and killed by a lorry whilst saving a child. This wasn't his only heroic deed of the day as after his death the hospital staff discovered his donor card, whipped out his kidneys and donated them for transplant.

This prompted a brief wave of sympathy for Debs, but she didn't grieve for too long, and within a couple of months was making plays for Willmott-Brown and for Colin – although she was successful with neither, for different reasons. Having failed to elicit sympathy as a merry widow, Debs's days on the Square were numbered.

Also...

▶ Mark turns up in Southend, living with a woman and her two children... ▶ The Square is threatened by protection racketeers and gangsters – the notorious 'Firm'... ▶ Sue has a phantom pregnancy and becomes desperate to adopt... ▶ Mary ditches her punk look in an attempt to win Andy, then has a brief affair with Mehmet... ▶ Lofty starts doing kissograms dressed as Carmen Miranda... ▶ Little Willy goes missing, but mercifully turns up in the company of a shady Latvian gentleman... ▶ Kathy holds a frilly knickers party... ▶ Pauline wins a Glamorous Granny competition... ▶ Sharon gets religion (but not for long)... ▶ A mugger stalks Walford... ▶ Roly gets sick from eating rat poison... ▶ Colin gets cold feet about having barrow-boy Barry moving in with him...

EVERYONE TALKED ABOUT...

Happy Christmas, darlin'

You can't say that Angie Watts didn't work at her marriage. After a year in which she'd conned her husband into believing that she had an incurable illness, she had every right to believe that she'd be rewarded with a bit of togetherness in the festive season. How wrong she was. Despite much wheedling in the back passage of the Vic, Den served her with divorce papers on Christmas Day – and 30 million viewers tuned in to watch Angie's humiliation.

▶ The clinging body language, the puppy-dog eyes – Angie drops the dignity in a last-ditch effort to save her marriage

▶ Den announces that he has a special Christmas present for Angie – something she wasn't expecting

▶ 'Happy Christmas, darlin''... and it's not a card in that envelope

▶ The 'duff-duff-duff' moment, as Angie goes into shock

1987

Angie and Den

The highlight of Christmas 1986 couldn't help but carry on as the biggest story of 1987, although in the aftermath of Den's decision to divorce Angie nothing could ever reach the same dramatic heights. The Watts spent the next 12 months alternately at each other's throats and wondering if they'd done the right thing after all. Angie announced her decision to take Den to the cleaners; Den retaliated by installing Jan behind the bar, only to realise that she was far too posh for the likes of him and giving her her marching orders in the summer.

Before long, Angie established herself as the chief barmaid of the rival Dagmar pub, managed by James Willmott-Brown, and put up with her ghastly yuppie clientele just for the pleasure of lording it over the Vic, which was floundering without her. But behind her brassy bar-room smiles, Angie was a wreck, drinking more heavily, going on silly shopping sprees 'on the plastic' and occasionally having to nip outside to throw up in the Square. Little wonder that Sharon was so distressed by her mother's behaviour that she dallied first with Simon Wicks, then with a clergyman called Duncan.

Den retaliated by having a string of flings, notably with a feisty caterer called Mags (whom Wicksy stole from him), and continued to moon over Michelle and his unacknowledged daughter. But it was clear to the great viewing public that Angie and Den were meant for each other, and so Sharon engineered a sneaky date which ended up with them in bed together again. Like two guilty teenagers, they decided to keep it quiet around the Square, but by the end of the year Angie quit the Dagmar and returned to the Vic – strictly as a business partner, you understand.

On the surface, 1987 ended on an up note for Angie and Den, but there was deep, dark trouble in store. Den was getting embroiled with 'The Firm', who paid off his debts on condition that he committed a string of offences for them. This involved running errands to Morocco, not to mention a spot of jury-nobbling – and, for Den, the writing was on the wall.

James Willmott-Brown (William Boyde) behind the Dagmar bar with Angie

Colin and Barry

Graphic designer Colin Russell and his barrow-boyfriend Barry Clark moved into Albert Square without much fanfare in 1986, but it was this year that their storylines started to dominate *EastEnders*, not to mention the national press. Less liberal characters like Pete Beale and Nick Cotton started to grumble about 'poofs' in the Square, while the papers went mad when Colin pecked Barry on the forehead.

They were never the likeliest of couples: class and age divided them, not to mention habits (Colin was fussy, Barry a slob) and ambitions (Barry wanted children, Colin did not). There were plenty of storylines involving them – Barry got involved with some petty crime, thanks to the bad influence of Nick Cotton, there was some minor fuss about a five-a-side football match and Colin's housework strike – but the real drama involved their relationship with the other residents of Albert Square. The more worldly women of Walford, like Angie, Pat and Kathy, had no problem about having gay neighbours and actually invited Colin's confidences. Dot, meanwhile, discovered the hideous truth while employed as Colin's cleaner, and started telling anyone who would listen that she was terrified of getting Aids.

Gradually, even Dot got used to the idea and accepted that Barry and Colin were little different from anyone else in Walford. Things took a nasty turn at the end of the year, when a burglary left Colin at the mercy of some seriously homophobic police officers who hinted that they might prosecute him for underage sex (even though Barry was, by this time, over 21 – the age of consent back in 1987).

Finally, the differences between the pair proved too great to overcome, and they agreed to go their separate ways at the end of 1987, after spending one final, sad New Year's Eve together.

Oh no, not my baby: Lofty with Michelle and Vicki

Michelle and Lofty

There was a serious competition going on in *EastEnders* in 1987: who, out of Michelle and Pauline, could be the most miserable woman in Walford? Michelle probably took the prize, but only just. Marriage to Lofty wasn't turning out to be a bed of roses, and for an intelligent 18-year-old with ambitions and energy it soon became clear that there was more to life than playing happy families with an unemployable asthmatic whose idea of splashing out was to buy a Family Railcard.

As the year wore on, Lofty became more and more interested in having a child of his own, and put pressure on Michelle not only to get pregnant, but also to allow him to adopt Vicki. Michelle had other ideas, and scuttled round to the Vic for one more crack at Den, offering to run away with him and Vicki to start a brand new life. It took Den mere seconds to decide that this was not a good idea.

Minor, irritating rows between Lofty and Michelle became as regular a feature of Walford life as the number 15 bus, and the only person who paid any attention was eagle-eyed Pauline, who soon figured out what was really going on. The year ended with Michelle telling her mother (rather than her husband) that she was expecting a second child. She was, predictably, not happy about it.

Pauline and Arthur

Pauline had troubles of her own – when didn't she? – having to deal with a mentally ill husband, pressing financial difficulties, an ailing mother (Lou kept having nasty turns), a delinquent son, an illegitimate granddaughter and a dangerous penchant for drab knitwear. Little wonder, then, that Pauline had a minor breakdown herself in the middle of the year and started fencing dodgy meat for Dennis Watts. It's the nearest Pauline ever came to a life of crime, and she pulled back from the brink at the eleventh hour when Michelle reminded her what a life of crime had done to Arthur and Mark.

Arthur went into hospital suffering from depression, and came out again just in time to be sent to prison for a month for the Christmas Club theft. When he came out, reliable Arthur promptly got into trouble with a loan shark, leaving viewers wondering why Pauline didn't just bash him over the head and be done with it. She did have a glimmer of how different life could be when she met an attractive man called Derek, but loyalty to her old man nipped any notions of adultery in the bud. At least Mark turned up for Christmas – and that's all Pauline ever truly seemed to want.

Arthur on the edge of a nervous breakdown

Mary

After dabbling with prostitution at the end of 1986, Mary flung herself wholeheartedly on to the game this year, with the result that Little Annie was frequently left home alone. The timely intervention of Arthur prevented the baby from being burned alive when a blanket fell on to the electric fire; this action alone justified Arthur's existence in Albert Square. Mary's parents turned up and bundled Little Annie off to Stockport.

Mary with Rod Norman (Christopher McHallem)

This shocked Mary into cleaning up her act (she was probably fed up of being beaten up by rival prostitutes anyway), in which she was considerably helped by the arrival of Rod the Roadie, an amiable drifter with a taste for feckless women. He helped her sort her life out and get Annie back – which, after a long battle with her parents and the social services, she finally did. Annie ended a dangerous year by nearly getting killed in a car crash, thanks to her drunken grandad, but lived to tell the tale.

EVERYONE TALKED ABOUT…

EastEnders' first gay kiss

It's hard to believe, but back in 1987 the sight of two men kissing was enough to undermine the very fabric of our society. Colin and Barry weren't the first gay characters in a British soap – *Brookside* had that distinction – but they were on primetime BBC1, and thus their power to corrupt and deprave was that much greater. The press reacted with 'outrage' and 'fury' at this 'filth' and, for a while, dubbed the show '*EastBenders*'.

Colin the graphic designer moves in on Barry the barrow boy, unaware that they're bringing down western civilisation

A chaste peck on the forehead – and Barry doesn't even stop drinking his tea! But the damage is done

Colin readjusts himself as the BBC switchboard goes into meltdown and the journalists start sharpening their pens

Later on, a steamy bed scene confirms the fact that *EastEnders* has lost all moral sense

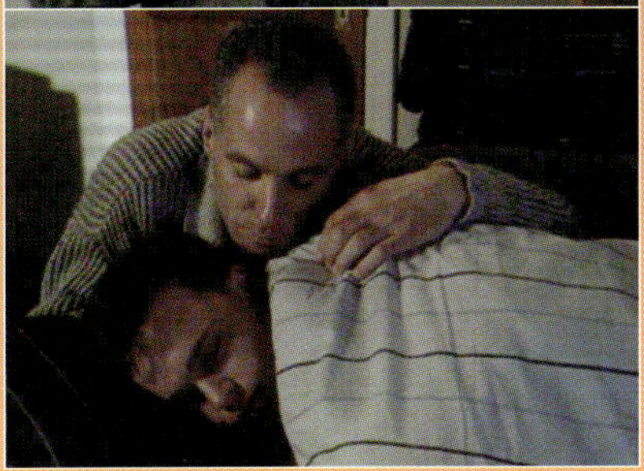

1987

From left to right: Barry Clark (Gary Hailes), Colin Russell (Michael Cashman), Arthur, Pauline, Ian, Pete, Den, Lou and Dot, enjoy a cockney singsong with Simon at the piano

The Walford Attacker

For several months the women of Walford could not walk the streets at night without falling prey to a maniac who started the year with a go at Sharon, then struck at Pat, whom he robbed and nearly killed. For a moment, nearly every male EastEnder was in the frame – Tony, Den, Wicksy and Pete all had to establish alibis. They were all finally cleared when plucky Debbie Wilkins used her martial-arts expertise to bag the real Walford Attacker, but not before Pete had managed to beat up a policeman.

Also...

▶ Kathy learns that her daughter wants to get in touch with her – but little do we know (yet) that it's Donna, one of the new girls on the block... ▶ Lofty's Auntie Irene dies in a hospice... ▶ Mehmet's wife and children turn up in the Square and lose their pet boa constrictor, Crush... ▶ Ali tries to have an affair with every woman in the Square, before patching up his marriage to Sue... ▶ Charlie and Nick Cotton both turn up to sponge off Dot at the same time... ▶ Charlie poisons everyone with some knock-off salmon... ▶ Pat meets up with an old flame by the name of Frank Butcher, who proposes marriage... ▶ Hannah leaves Tony, who returns to Trinidad... ▶ A camera crew makes a patronising TV documentary about East End life... ▶ Little Willy gets sick from eating a newspaper...

1988

Cindy Williams (Michelle Collins) rides into town

Kathy and Donna

Kathy Beale stepped into the spotlight for most of 1988 – a year that would put her through practically all of the ordeals that female soap stars can face. The year didn't start badly: Kathy had lost her job at the Vic, but was quickly snapped up at a rival establishment, where she rather enjoyed the attentions of the friendly owner, James Willmott-Brown. The only cloud on the horizon came in the shape of the strange Donna Ludlow, a young woman who had turned up in the Square in 1987 and seemed determined to get to know Kathy.

It didn't take long for Donna to explain her interest: she was none other than Kathy's daughter, given up for adoption as a baby. To her surprise, she got a frosty reception from Mummy – who, pushed into a corner by her manipulative and needy daughter, eventually confronted her with the truth. Donna was unhinged by the news that she was conceived as the result of rape, and spent the rest of the year in a downward spiral. She started going out with Simon Wicks, who was busily working his way through the entire female population of Albert Square, and ended up having the odd tussle with his other girlfriends, notably slap-happy Cindy. For a moment it looked as if she would start going out with Ian, until she warned him off by telling him that their relationship would amount to incest.

Eventually Donna ran out of friends around the Square, and started sleeping wherever she could find a place to lay her head. A stay with Michelle and Sharon ended abruptly when she tried to break up their friendship, and Donna ended up living in the Albert Square squat, where, inevitably, she became a drug addict immediately. From there it was a rapid decline, and Donna ended the year hooked on heroin and prostituting herself to support her habit. Rod the Roadie, who no longer had Mary to look after, tried to straighten her out, but to little effect. Donna's days were numbered.

Kathy's Rape

No sooner had Kathy been confronted with an unwelcome reminder of her rape at the age of 14, than she had to contend with something even more hideous. Willmott-Brown had taken a smarmy, unhealthy interest in Kathy from the first day of her employment at the Dagmar, thinking up little ruses to engineer more time with her. Pete reacted to the obvious infatuation by telling Kathy that she was behaving and dressing like a tart – which had the predictable result of pushing her closer to Willmott-Brown. The stage was set for a crime that rocked the Square.

By the summer, Willmott-Brown was hanging around Kathy more and more, confiding in her about his ex-wife, buying her expensive birthday presents and generally getting on her nerves. Then, one night in July, when Kathy had had yet another row with Pete, Willmott-Brown invited her to his flat for a drink

Willmott-Brown, the yuppie from hell

– and raped her. Kathy, bruised and in shock, was discovered by Den, who immediately vowed revenge.

Willmott-Brown's pub was burned to the ground, and he fled to Nottingham to start a new life, far from vengeful East End gangsters. But Kathy's ordeal was just beginning. In the aftermath of the rape, she became depressed and isolated from her husband – who, to make matters worse, was never convinced that she was entirely blameless in the affair. He took her on holiday to Majorca, but even that didn't help; when they returned to the Square, they were more estranged than ever. Pete started drinking, Pauline started interfering, and just when it seemed that things couldn't get any worse, Willmott-Brown returned to the Square to persuade Kathy to drop the rape charges. The year ended on a cliffhanger: would she accept his offer of £5000, or would she continue to seek justice?

The End of Michelle's Marriage

Furious at her mother for telling Lofty that she was pregnant, Michelle retaliated by terminating the pregnancy. This was the final straw in her marriage to Lofty, who wisely decided he wanted nothing more to do with the Beales or the Fowlers, and left Walford to start a job as a handyman in a children's care home in Bedfordshire. His early-morning flit was witnessed only by Den, taking Roly for a walk.

Michelle got a job as a receptionist for Dr Legg, and moved out of the family home to share a flat with Sharon.

Sharon and Michelle: the big hair years

Who is Wicksy's Father?

If ever there was a woman with a past in Walford, it was Pat Wicks. Less than a year after her return, the whole of Albert Square was exercising itself over one burning question: who was the real father of Simon Wicks? Pete had always believed Simon to be his, legally conceived during wedlock. Pat, however, let it be known that in fact the father was Kenny, Pete's brother, who had been bundled off to New Zealand to conceal his guilt. Kenny turned up in the Square in 1988, leading to tense confrontations all round – not to mention some very understandable confusion on the part of poor Simon, who comforted himself by having sex with a large number of women. At a critical point, claiming that she really couldn't remember who the father was, Pat even suggested that Den could be in the frame, and went so far as attempting to blackmail him.

After causing maximum distress to all and sundry, Pat finally confessed that Wicksy was a Wicks after all, without a drop of Beale blood in his veins. She confessed to Lou that she had only ever spread the rumour as a way of getting control over the men in her life.

Pat and Frank

Redemption, for Pat Wicks, came in the bulky form of Frank Butcher, the only man she'd ever loved, who had thrust her into the arms of Pete Beale when he'd refused to marry her all those years ago. Frank turned up in the Square after the death of his first wife, and his two teenage children, Ricky and Diane, joined him shortly after. The spark was still there with Pat, and before you knew it they were scheming to wrest the tenancy of the Queen Vic from Den and Angie – who had decided to up and sell anyway.

After months of waiting, and a considerable amount of bribery, Pat and Frank got the Vic, thus beginning a new era in Albert Square. Ricky and Diane moved in, adopted Roly and immediately added their own unique brand of romantic ineptitude to Walford's younger generation. And it wasn't just kids that Frank brought with him: by the end of the year his tyrannical mother, Mo, had moved into number 23 and was attempting to run her son's life.

Den and The Firm

Den finally got his come-uppance for all that dirtiness when he got in much deeper with local gangsters The Firm than he could really handle. Angie left Walford at the beginning of the year to start a new life in Spain – leaving Den with no option but to surrender his beloved pub to Frank and Pat, and to start a new life as the puppet manager of Strokes Wine Bar (formerly Henry's), a front for The Firm.

Incensed by Kathy's rape, Den persuaded Brad from The Firm to 'torch' the Dagmar, and watched with glee as his hated rival's pub burned to the ground. Little did he know, however, that his problems were just beginning. The Firm's boss, the sinister Mr Vinnicombe, decided it would be better if Den were to take the rap for the fire and 'disappear' for a while, with a hefty pay-off. Den relocated to Manchester, but quickly got wind of The Firm's plans to silence him forever and opted instead to hand himself in at the nearest police station.

For the rest of the year, we saw Den only as an inmate of Dickens Hill prison, which became the setting for an almost entirely separate spin-off soap opera. Den suffered beatings when The Firm suspected him of having grassed them up to the police, but eventually he persuaded his former associates of his innocence, in that matter at least, and was left unmolested to become 'Number 1 of the Landing'.

Colin

At the start of the year, Barry told Colin that he'd decided to 'go straight', and left Walford to pursue a career as a DJ on a cruise liner. Colin pined for a while, and started to feel under the weather, a situation that was not helped when he was beaten up by two strangers. After inexplicably losing the use of

1988

Family man Frank Butcher (Mike Reid) with children Diane (Sophie Lawrence) and Ricky (Sid Owen) and new wife Pat – and not forgetting Roly, the pub dog

his legs, Colin reported to Dr Legg's surgery and Legg diagnosed multiple sclerosis, although he thought it advisable to keep the truth from his patient.

Colin ended the year with a new boyfriend, Guido, but would leave the show in 1989 to face a rapid decline in health.

Also

▶ Ian starts going out with Kenny's daughter, his cousin Elizabeth, but she's just using him… ▶ Mary becomes addicted to speed, goes back on the game and then leaves Walford for good… ▶ Angie suffers kidney failure and has to start dialysis… ▶ Angie recuperates in Spain, where she falls in love with Sonny… ▶ Roly goes missing but is found, safe and sound… ▶ Sue gives birth to a baby boy, Ali Junior… ▶ Tom drops dead in the Vic toilets… ▶ Charlie Cotton returns, steals from Dot and disappears… ▶ Lou says her farewells to her family and dies the next day…

Duncan (David Gillespie), the amorous vicar, leads the mourners at Lou's funeral

EVERYONE TALKED ABOUT…

The rape

It was one of *EastEnders*' most contentious storylines, setting the seal on the show's reputation for hard-hitting drama and drawing criticisms of sensationalism. We knew Willmott-Brown was a villain from the first moment he walked on to the Square – well, he was middle class, after all – but when his frustrated passion for Kathy spilled over into violence, the viewers went into shock. *EastEnders* would tackle the subject of rape again, but never to such devastating effect.

▶ It started innocently enough: Kathy came up to Willmott-Brown's bachelor pad for wine and sympathy after a row with Pete

▶ The big-haired seducer makes his move, telling Kathy how much he loves her

▶ Kathy realises that W-B will not take no for an answer, and starts to fight back

▶ The aftermath – and the real beginning of Kathy's troubles. By the end of the year, her marriage was on the rocks

1989

Den's 'Death'

After months of uncertainty in his dealings with The Firm, Den finally realised that they did not, after all, have his best interests at heart. Word reached him in prison that his 'insurance' – the papers that he had lodged with a solicitor proving The Firm's guilt in the burning of the Dagmar – had been stolen and destroyed. Den was no fool, and had a spare copy in reserve, and so The Firm decided, after all, that the only good Den was a dead Den.

Sprung from a van on his way to trial, Den was suddenly about to face a much rougher form of justice, but managed to evade the clutches of the menacing Mr Mantel and go on the run. He might have made good his escape had it not been for Michelle, who started asking a lot of awkward questions of any Firm member who crossed her path, awakening them to the fact that she could just be the vital clue in their hunt for the missing Den.

And so all roads led, with tragic inevitability, to that notorious canalside rendezvous, when Michelle poured out her heart to Den, told him that she would wait for him and that, one day, they would be together with little Vicki as a family. Den made all the right noises, although we knew that this was the last thing he wanted. Michelle headed back to the Square, leaving Den face to face with a man and a gun concealed in a bunch of daffodils. A shot is fired – and Mantel, watching through binoculars, mutters 'Bye, bye, Den...'

And so began one of *EastEnders*' longest-running mysteries: did Den die that day by the canal? Police forensics suggested that the blood found on the bank matched Den's, and announced that they were 99 per cent certain he was dead. A body was found a year later and never identified.

Sharon was distraught, of course, but couldn't understand why her friend Michelle was taking the news so badly. With her usual sense of timing, Michelle chose this moment to tell Sharon that Den was, after all, the father of her baby – which made them family, didn't it? Sharon didn't take the news as well as Michelle had hoped, and threw her out of the flat before storming round to the Fowlers to announce that the £9500 Den had left for 'his daughter' was, by rights, Vicki's. And so slow-witted Arthur finally learned the truth about Michelle's pregnancy, reacting with his usual impotent rage. Michelle and Sharon remained at daggers drawn for a while, tossing the £9500 inheritance to and fro like a hot potato. It took little Vicki to contract meningitis before they realised that friendship was more important than a small thing like having sex with other people's fathers.

Den's final day?

Cindy, Ian and Wicksy

Not satisfied with life as a simple market trader on an East End hat stall, Cindy decided to cause maximum disruption in Walford by engineering one of the most painful love triangles ever seen in

Ian and Cindy celebrate their engagement. Inset: a cockney ménage à trois*: the happy couple and best man (to both of them) Simon*

EastEnders. She started the year half-heartedly going out with Ian, who was never going to be the right man for her; he was always more interested in his dull plans for taking over the café than he was in satisfying Cindy's gargantuan sexual appetite. Matters were not helped by the fact that Wicksy, who was more truly her match, was interested in settling down with Sharon, whom he had comforted after Den's disappearance. Their friendly relationship rapidly developed into something much more serious, leaving Cindy fuming on the sidelines and agreeing to marry Ian more out of spite than anything else. The fact that Ian chose to celebrate the engagement with a party in the café proved that he was a total romantic dud.

Finally, after one too many rebuffs from foolish Ian, Cindy managed to catch Wicksy on his own at the pub and get her wicked way once more – only to fall instantly and inevitably pregnant. This was bad enough, but when Ian started announcing that he didn't really want children (because they are too expensive, of course), Cindy was thrown into a spin. Unwilling to have an abortion (she was a good Catholic in that respect, if in no other), Cindy tried every trick in the book to get Wicksy back – right down to secreting one of her earrings in his shirt pocket for Sharon to find. That backfired, leaving Cindy with no option other than to tell the truth – a course of action she never had much taste for. She informed Wicksy that he was about to be a daddy, but of course he didn't believe her. She'd cried 'wolf' once too often.

Throughout the summer and autumn, Ian went ahead blithely making plans for the wedding while Cindy wrestled with her conscience. After a final confrontation with Simon, who rejected her outright, Cindy agreed to marry Ian, only to spoil the day by having a huge row with her new father-in-law and ending up in tears at her own reception. The pattern was set for the married life of Mr and Mrs Beale.

When the baby was born on Boxing Day, a few wiser heads around the Square did some quick sums and realised that, if Ian was the father, little Stephen must be somewhat premature. The year ended with Ian proudly toasting the future while his wife and best man looked forward to the 90s with some misgivings…

Kathy and Pete

In one final act of revenge, Kathy lulled Willmott-Brown into believing that she was ready to take his hush money and drop the rape charges – only to betray him straight into the hands of a listening DI Ashley, who dragged him off to face prison. After a hideous trial, Willmott-Brown was found guilty and disappeared for good.

Sadly, this was not the beginning of a happy ending for Kathy and Pete. She could never forgive him for his shoddy treatment of her in the aftermath of the attack and so he began drinking more heavily to assuage the pain of a dissolving marriage. By the spring, Pete was sleeping in the lock-up, contemplating suicide and/or murder. He hit rock bottom when, in a drunken frenzy, he crashed a car and nearly killed Roly. There was no other option for the scriptwriters but to pack him off to New Zealand for a few weeks.

Kathy wasn't idle in his absence, and fell for the smarmy charms of Laurie Bates, the new fruit-and-veg man on the market. Pete wasn't best pleased to find that she was fraternising with the enemy, but produced his own love interest in the shape of Barbara, a woman he'd met in New Zealand. It was a bluff; Pete wanted Kathy back as much as ever, but she made it abundantly clear that she, at least, had moved on, if only to a veg stall a bit further up Bridge Street.

The Death of Donna

Donna Ludlow went from bad to worse in 1989, thieving from the market in order to finance her galloping drug habit, and attempting to blackmail Ali, who had foolishly slept with her in 1988. Rod rescued her from a particularly nasty gang rape, and attempted to straighten her out, but he was even less successful with Donna than he had been with Mary. Donna, feeling that she just wasn't getting enough attention in the Square, announced to everyone that her parents had been killed in a car crash. Just as she was basking in a warm glow of sympathy in the Vic, her mother walked in.

This was the beginning of the end for Donna, as all her neighbours, with the exception of kind-hearted Dot, turned their backs on her. She hit back by telling Sue the truth about Ali, destroying that already-rocky marriage in one fell swoop. Rod had soon had enough, and left her to her own devices. Even Kathy, Donna's birth mother, didn't want to know. And so Donna finally flipped, had a moment of madness on Dot's sofa, took an overdose and choked to death on her own vomit. Her passing was mourned by none; even Kathy seemed to get over it pretty quickly.

Sue and Ali never recovered from the blow inflicted by Ali's infidelity. Sue snatched baby Ali, only to have him snatched back by Ali Senior as she was visiting Hassan's grave. Distressed to have lost not one but two children, Sue broke down and started pouring earth over her head. She was later picked up in a bewildered state and sectioned in a psychiatric hospital. Ali, after getting into more and more trouble around the Square, finally ran amok with a crowbar and was taken away by some Turkish-Cypriot relatives, to the unspeakable relief of his neighbours.

Pat and Frank

It was only a matter of time before propinquity got the better of Pat and Frank, and in June they were married in true cockney style, driving out of Albert Square in a totter's cart complete with a pearly king. It was a brief moment of happiness: within a month, Pat had become stepmother to five-year-old Janine, the child from hell. Janine, Frank's daughter by his previous wife, was a bedwetter, a sleepwalker, a compulsive liar and a self-harmer with a taste for

EVERYONE TALKED ABOUT...

On the waterfront

Nobody could quite remember why Den was in so much trouble with The Firm – all that mattered was that there were a number of people who wanted him dead. Sprung from prison and on the run, Den faced destiny in the unlikely shape of a young man carrying a bunch of daffodils. There was a bang and a splash, but, despite a great deal of dredging, Den's body was never found. For the next 14 years, we lived in the vague hope that, somehow, he would re-emerge.

Fresh from a heart-to-heart with Michelle, Den walks away to start a new life far from Walford

Ah! Young lovers, enjoying the scenic delights of a polluted canal in a desolate part of the East End. But wait...

That's not a daffodil. Look out, Den...

Job done – or so The Firm thinks. But it takes more than a canalside hitman to put Den Watts out of action

Would you buy a car from these people? Frank and Pat open the car lot for business

running out in front of cars. She stole from Pat, then ran away from home, taking her Bros poster with her, only to be found sleeping in the back of a parked Dormobile, where she would have been better left. Frank's response to this catalogue of bad behaviour was to bribe Janine with presents rather than discipline her. Little wonder that she ended up dabbling in the world of drugs and prostitution.

The year closed with Pat and Frank buying the B&B across the Square from the pub, while Frank opened a used car lot and got immediately involved in a ringing scandal. Theirs was not a quiet life.

Also...

▶ Colin discovers that he has MS, and goes to live with his brother in Bristol... ▶ The Queen Vic extends its opening hours to all-day drinking... ▶ Ricky starts hanging out with a bad crowd of racists, and fails all his GCSEs... ▶ Ethel's admirer Benny Bloom proposes to her, then drops dead, leaving her £2000... ▶ Carmel marries Matthew, who immediately starts beating her up and then gets stabbed... ▶ Pauline gets knocked down by Ricky, the hospital staff discover she has fibroids, and, after an extended break in Leigh-on-Sea, she has a hysterectomy over Christmas... ▶ Sharon becomes a compulsive shopper... ▶ Nick Cotton's 'wife' Hazel cons money out of Dot, then starts going out with Rod... ▶ Charlie Cotton is revealed as a bigamist... ▶ Michelle confirms her taste for married men with a new boyfriend, Danny...

War of the Words

EastEnders clocks up over two hundred episodes a year – that's a lot of stories and characters to develop. The key to keeping it fresh and up-to-date is the script behind it. For each episode, the show's writers interweave up to half a dozen storylines involving a cast of over 40 principal characters, all of which have to be put across to viewers in a direct and recognisably _EastEnders_ style.

The writing process is highly organised, and has grown out of the pooled skills of a group of core writers and producers with, between them, vast experience of continuing drama. Quarterly planning meetings form the backbone of the process; the main creative team goes away for a few days to discuss long-term goals and to review suggestions or developments that may have been under consideration for some time. It's here that the big decisions are made: new characters are created, old characters are axed, major bombshells are planned and the big events of the year (particularly Christmas) are pencilled in well in advance. No one

'Clans were the original building-blocks of *EastEnders*, and that's what the show is returning to now.'

knows this better than Louise Berridge, who steered *EastEnders* through two years as executive producer, from 2002 to 2004. 'When you're planning a show like *EastEnders*, you could be looking up to five years ahead,' she says. 'You talk about where you want the show to be in the future, how you should change the basic structure; you always have to keep your eye on long-term goals as well as short-term story development.'

It was at one such meeting that the decision was made, for instance, to bring back Den Watts in 2003 – part of a long-term policy of strengthening family groups in *EastEnders*. 'Clans were the original building-blocks of *EastEnders*, and that's what the show is returning to now,' says Berridge. 'When it started, it was all about the Watts, the Fowlers, the Wicks and the Beales. For a while, that focus was lost; there were too many single characters hanging around on the periphery of the action, while the family groups were being weakened and compromised. Then the Slaters were brought in as a big, powerful clan, and the Watts family was rebuilt. The Fowlers were reconstituted in 2004, as were the Beales and the Mitchells. Those families are the mainspring of most of the best drama, because once you've got family groups you instantly have conflicts of loyalty. It was important to make a link between the Slaters and the Watts, for instance – hence Dennis and Zoe's relationship. That's a situation that will create a lot of drama in the future.'

Once the bigger picture has been established in the quarterly conference, the writers get together in monthly script sessions during which four weeks' worth of stories are worked out in detail and assigned to individuals. From that point on, it's up to the writers to breathe life into situations and characters within the well-defined parameters of Albert Square. But don't be fooled into thinking that the creative process behind *EastEnders* is an exact science. 'There's always been a lot of personal input

'When the show started, it was all about the Watts, the Fowlers, the Wicks and the Beales.'

into the show,' says John Yorke, for many years an *EastEnders* script editor and, between 2000 and 2002, executive producer. 'When I was writing stories for the show, I'd sit down at my computer on a Monday morning and ring up all my friends to see what had happened to them over the weekend. I'd have a good gossip, get all the juiciest stories and then just change the names to Michelle and Sharon.'

With the show's growth to its current four-times-a-week size, strategies have been developed to streamline the writing process. 'Characters always used to be created on paper first,' says Tony Jordan, a veteran *EastEnders* writer who is now the series consultant, with special responsibility for storylining. 'We'd talk about characters, then the writers would come up with a biography for them, and we'd start writing scripts. Because we work so far in advance, we were often writing lines long before the part had been cast. We were working in a vacuum, because we didn't have a face or a voice to write to, and that's very difficult. It used to take a while for the actors and the characters to gel. Now we've reversed that process, and every time we're introducing major characters we work with the actors first.'

Out of this difficulty arose the highly successful process of actors' workshops, which were introduced in 2002. 'John Yorke and I knew that we wanted to introduce a big new family,' says Jordan, 'but that was all we knew. So we called up a lot of casting agents and got them to send us actors that we would want to work with. We put them all into rehearsal rooms for three days, took them through a lot of improvisations and just watched what happened. After that we kept a few and let a lot go, and carried on doing more improvisations, trying out different combinations. That was when the stars started to emerge – Laila Morse, Jessie Wallace, Elaine Lordan, Kacey Ainsworth. All the best actors were women, and we developed the idea of a family dominated by women. So the Slater girls were born.'

As soon as casting and characters had been decided on, videos were sent to all the writers so that they could start working directly for the people concerned. 'It's better all round,' says Jordan. 'As a writer, you have a face and a voice in front of you, which is a much better starting point than two sheets of A4 paper. And it's better for the actors too, because they're playing to their strengths. The best *EastEnders* performances have always come from actors who are basically playing themselves. Martin Kemp didn't have to try too hard to be Steve Owen – he's a sharp lad, suited and booted with that edge of danger to him. The same applies to Ross Kemp and Steve McFadden as the Mitchell boys. There's no point in casting against type in a soap, because if you've got to inhabit that character all day every day you need to be able to do it very instinctively.'

Once characters are set, it's just a question of finding situations in which to place them. It's often been said of *EastEnders* that the same basic plots are recycled again and again for different sets of characters – and that's all part of the plan. 'Our material is the stuff of real life,' says Jordan. 'We're writing about realistic characters in a realistic part of London, and we're reflecting what goes on in places like that. We're never going to depart from realism; there will never be UFOs landing in Albert Square, or alien abductions. Our subject matter is the minutiae of daily life: pregnancy, infidelity, parenting, money problems. Those things don't change much from one generation to the next. Attitudes do change, so each time we return to one of those topics they'll be treated in a different way – but the basic fabric of day-to-day life hasn't really changed. The themes of drama are the same now as they ever were.'

One thing that has changed, however, is the skill with which that raw material is handled. *EastEnders* has always striven to be character-led, rather than dominated by issues – and that strength is being played to more and more. 'The secret of a good

Sending East End boys into a spin: the Slater girls

'The secret of a good *EastEnders* story is the length of time over which it grows.'

EastEnders story is the length of time over which it grows,' says Jordan. 'The unique thing about soap is that you can plant a story and then wait months before you deliver it. When we introduced the Slater family, we all knew that Kat was Zoe's mother – but we waited 18 months before we let the audience in on it. During that time they'd got to know the Slaters, they'd learned to like them and they'd made a certain investment in them – so when the truth came out, they were willing to go on a very tough journey with them. We went for an emotional connection with the characters first, then we hit the viewers with the big story. If we'd introduced the story at the same time as we introduced the family, the reaction would have been very different. The characters would have been defined by the issues, rather than vice versa.'

The same is true of all the great *EastEnders* storylines: Angie and Den's divorce, for instance, which came at the end of the show's second year, but which had been planned from the very beginning. Sharongate, another highlight, was allowed to mature for months before the explosive revelations in the Vic. Long-term planning is the key to this kind of dramatic time bomb. 'The hardest thing, sometimes, is knowing how a certain story will end. We're trying, now, to look at characters in terms of their long-term story – of getting them to a certain point where they've reached a conclusion. That's when you have to take the tough decision of saying goodbye. But those stories can take a very long time to work out. It's hard to plan for the very long term these days, because the longest any actor will sign up for is about three years, but we have to keep the bigger picture in mind. Take the character of Dennis, for instance. He's a murderer – and so we know that his overall story, basically, is a road to redemption. That could take a lifetime to reach, but when he reaches it, his story is closed.'

1990

Diane Runs Away

Diane Butcher had every reason to be fed up at home. Her mother had died, she'd inherited Pat as a stepmother, and she was forced to share a room with Janine, the brat from hell. And so it came as little surprise when, on the evening of her birthday in January, she decided to run away from home. Ricky hadn't helped matters by concealing her birthday cards – this was one of the many 'surprise parties' in *EastEnders* that had disastrous consequences. Diane disappeared into the night, unaware that her friends and family were waiting for her at the Community Centre.

Diane's disappearance sent the remaining Butchers into a tailspin. Frank made several frantic trips to Leeds, believing Diane to be hiding out with her on/off boyfriend Paul – but Paul knew nothing of her, having wisely split up with her some months before. Things got nasty when a young girl's body was found in Leeds, but, mercifully, it turned out not to be Diane's. Frank returned to London, and showed his relief by slapping Ricky about a bit.

Eventually, after two months of radio silence, Diane phoned home to let Frank know that she was alive and well, and finally agreed to meet him at King's Cross station. As Frank drove his errant chick back to Walford we learned – in a very rare *EastEnders* flashback – what exactly had befallen Diane in her months away from home. Inevitably, she had fallen in with a bad lot, notably Disa O'Brien, a runaway who tried to lure her into prostitution to raise the money for a flat, and Matthew Taylor, a dodgy artist who persuaded Diane to model nude for him. Frank's only concern seemed to be that Diane hadn't done anything to embarrass him in her absence, and he proceeded to treat her even worse than he had before she ran away.

Taylor was soon sniffing around Walford, leaving embarrassing tokens of his regard for Diane – like a life-size nude statue right in the middle of Albert Square. He was given his marching orders soon enough, but not before he'd tempted Diane to live in Spain with the promise of free art lessons. During her months on the street, Diane had learned that what she really wanted out of life was to become a photographer, or a graffiti artist, or anything that allowed her to express her deep dissatisfaction with being Frank Butcher's daughter. As a result she started hanging around in public libraries, bringing bagladies back to the B&B and doing hideous murals (works of art in her eyes) on any available wall. And just to complicate her life even further, she started seeing the newly returned Mark Fowler.

Diane, down and out in King's Cross

Diane's year ended as strangely as it had begun, when Disa dumped an unwanted baby on her doorstep on Christmas Day.

Cindy, Ian and Simon

The big scandal of 1990 revolved, predictably, around Cindy. She started off with the best of intentions, settling down to happy family life with Ian and baby Steven, telling Simon (the child's real father) to sling his hook and leave them in peace. Simon suddenly discovered a paternal instinct, however, and started hanging around the child and buying expensive presents – always a sure sign of concealed parenthood in Walford. He cornered Cindy at every opportunity, telling her that he had made a big mistake – and, inevitably, their whisperings were overheard, first by Michelle in the Square and then later by Kathy in an unforgettable scene involving a baby alarm.

All of this attention was too much for Cindy, who got quickly bored with being Mrs Ian Beale and started to realise that her true vocation was that of homewrecker. When Simon chucked Sharon and declared his intentions, Cindy couldn't resist, and suddenly found herself promising to tell Ian the truth and start a new life with Simon and the baby. This proved to be more than she could manage – but she did let slip that Ian wasn't Steven's daddy, which was a start. Ian didn't take the news well; in fact, he drove off in a violent rage, crashed the van and busted his leg, in what may have been a suicide attempt. Recovering in hospital, he claimed to have forgotten the circumstances of his 'accident' – which was handy.

A rural idyll for Wicksy, Cindy and Steven

Cindy wasn't fooled, and decamped to her parents' house in Devon, where Simon joined her to play happy families. Their rural idyll was rudely interrupted when Ian came hobbling down the drive and lobbed his crutch through their window. Some tense negotiations sent him hobbling back to Walford – with Cindy's father's shotgun concealed in a bag.

Now that the identity of Steven's father was common knowledge, Albert Square could get its teeth into a good old-fashioned cockney feud. The Beales and the Fowlers started holding family conferences at the drop of a hat, and decided to boycott the Vic, where Wicksy was still working. Ian, who was fast developing a taste for grand theatrical gestures, threw Cindy's belongings out of the window and on to the street. The unrepentant lovers moved into the B&B and faced the music.

Ian stopped short of blowing Simon's head off, and dumped the gun in the canal instead. When blood tests confirmed that he was not, after all, Steven's father, he sought a more subtle form of revenge, framing Simon for a series of thefts from the pub till and then, when he was caught out, sabotaging Simon's van by draining off the brake fluid. Finally Simon and Cindy could stand it no longer, and left Walford on Steven's first birthday to start a new life far from the psychotic attentions of Ian Beale. It would be nice to say that they lived happily ever after – but, come on, this is *EastEnders*...

The Mitchells Arrive

Two beefy-looking brothers turned up in Albert Square in a white Porsche and, after a brief calm

Here comes trouble! The Mitchell siblings Grant (Ross Kemp), Sam (Danniella Westbrook) and Phil (Steve McFadden)

before the storm, started making themselves thoroughly unpopular. Phil and Grant Mitchell were petty criminals and car mechanics – useful when a bit of heavy work was required, like nicking documents from council offices, but bad news in terms of law and order. Arthur got drawn into their illegal schemes, but then he always was a sucker.

By the end of the year, they were well and truly established in Walford, ruling the roost from the Arches and making life hell for their oafish new employee, Ricky Butcher. He, however, was delighted when the youngest Mitchell turned up – a hard-faced blonde called Samantha, with whom he fell instantly in love. They snatched a few moments of happiness in the back of a clapped-out VW camper van, but it was hard for young love to bloom with Grant and Phil breathing down their necks. Grant, however, wasn't averse to a bit of romance, and started going out with an eager Sharon.

Dot and Nick

Nick Cotton returned to Walford, claiming to be a reformed character. He had found Christ, he told anyone who'd listen, and was no longer interested in murder and thieving. Dot fell for it, of course, and welcomed the prodigal son with open arms, particularly as he seemed so keen to look after her. Within days Nick had taken over the running of the household, even going so far as to cook Dot healthy meals.

These turned out not to be so healthy after all. Dot started to sicken, and Ethel – who was right, for once – decided that Nick must be poisoning her in order to get his hands on her money (she'd had a small win on the *Walford Gazette* bingo). Could it be true? Would Nick really stoop that low? All was revealed when we learned that Dot had changed her will in favour of Nick's 'mission' – run by a bogus priest named Alastair – and that Nick was practising his mother's handwriting in order to forge a suicide note. Finally, Dot cottoned on and called Nick's bluff over a poisoned shepherd's pie. Nick, unable to

EVERYONE TALKED ABOUT…

That fateful baby alarm

The first rule of adultery: don't leave a baby alarm transmitting in a room where it might be heard by your mother-in-law. Cindy, heedless of this advice, carried on regardless with her paramour (also her half-brother-in-law). You can't really blame her: Wicksy was, after all, the father of her child, and was a much more appetising option than her real husband, Ian. Kathy took the news badly, but opted not to inform Ian what was going on, which made for bad blood in later weeks.

There's nothing quite like a bag of nappies to bring out the passionate side of a woman's nature

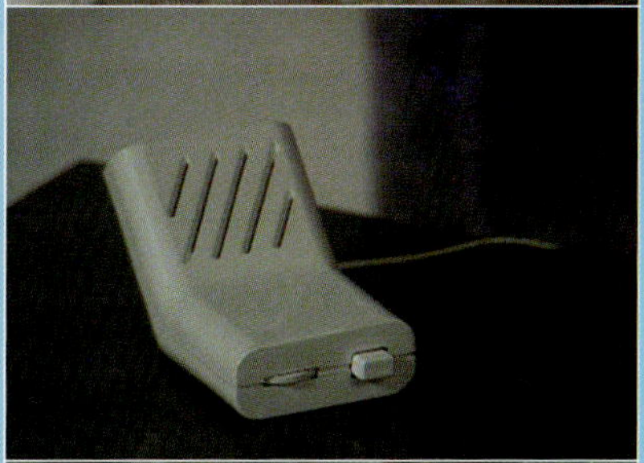

As Cindy and Wicksy get cosy in the bedroom, the baby alarm is relaying every sweet nothing to the rest of the house

'I say, the *Afternoon Play* is getting a bit racy these days…'

The penny drops, as Kathy hears things that baby alarms weren't designed for

watch in cold blood while his mother killed herself, fled the scene of the crime – and learned that Dot had changed her will once again, to benefit famine victims.

Sharon's Mother

Browsing around the market one day, Sharon found a signet ring that had belonged to Den. A little investigation traced it back to the canal bank, where a full-scale dredging operation turned up a body that could have been Den's. They buried it anyway, with full East End pomp and circumstance.

This seemed to tip Sharon over the edge. Rejected by Simon, she put all her energies into finding her birth mother, who turned out to be an uptight woman called Carol who didn't really want to know her long-lost daughter. Little wonder: Sharon was so intense by this time that even her best friend Michelle was starting to find her a bit creepy. Finally, after several abortive meetings, Sharon decided that she wasn't that interested in being Carol's daughter after all, and ended the year transferring her massive neediness to the broad shoulders of Grant Mitchell.

Mo's Dementia

Frank's mother Mo started to display symptoms of absent-mindedness – leaving taps running, causing floods, that sort of thing. Nobody thought much of it until her rapid deterioration in the spring, while Pat and Frank were on holiday. Mo's behaviour became stranger and stranger: sending birthday cards to long-dead relatives, dropping lighted fags into the laundry basket, chucking pasta shapes all over the kitchen floor. In her rare moments of lucidity, Mo revealed that she was terrified of meeting the same fate as her grandmother, who had died in a state of total dementia. She asked Frank to put her out of her misery, but he couldn't deliver the *coup de grâce*, and sent Mo off to live with his sister Joan in Colchester instead.

Celestine (Leroy Golding) and Etta Tavernier (Jacqui Gordon-Lawrence)

The Taverniers

Celestine and Etta Tavernier and their three children, Clyde, the oldest, and twins Hattie and Lloyd, moved into the Square in 1990, complete with their own family problems. Clyde was desperately missing his son Kofi, who was living with his grandparents in Bristol. Lloyd was getting ill with sickle-cell disease, and frightened everyone with a near-death experience in the autumn. Only Hattie seemed to be a happy child – but her time would come.

Clyde panicked when he learned that Kofi's grandparents were planning to take the child to live permanently in Jamaica, and so he tailed them to the airport, was reunited with Kofi, and brought him back to the Square on Christmas Day.

Also...

▶ Michelle suffers further indignities at the hands of married Danny, whom she finally chucks... ▶ Mark returns to Walford with a secret – which he won't even share with Michelle... ▶ Kathy chucks Laurie Bates, and starts going out with the new landlord at the Vic, Eddie Royle... ▶ Pete and Michelle lead a campaign to stop the council closing down the market... ▶ Arthur gets into trouble for working while signing on...

Matriarchs

Depending on your point of view, they're the warm-hearted cockney mother hens of a close-knit community, or a bunch of evil nags who delight in stirring up trouble.

Pauline Fowler

She's the Boadicea of the Battleaxes, a woman who will always leap to the worst conclusion and immediately start broadcasting her own dire prejudices. Pauline thinks of herself as a family woman, and yet she's done everything in her power to bust up the Fowler clan. Her abrasive nagging drove Arthur to despair, to adultery and, indirectly, to death. She harassed Michelle continuously until she fled to America. She sulked so often with Mark – refusing, till the last moment, to attend his last marriage – that he left Walford to die rather than being around her. And look at Martin: hardly a glowing advert for Pauline's parenting skills.

Peggy Mitchell (Butcher, Martin)

Second only to Pauline for consistent pompous negativity, Peggy has always assumed an almost papal infallibility. Whatever anybody does – particularly her own children – she knows better. And yet Peggy's own personal life is nothing short of a disaster, strewn with failed marriages, dismal affairs and a spectacularly awful brood of children. Peggy is also without doubt Walford's champion slapper: you name 'em, she's slapped 'em.

Dot Branning (Cotton)

A certain candidate for sainthood, Dot has put up with everything that life has to throw at her and still come back for more. Her husband Charlie was not only bigamous – he was also carrying on with her half-sister Rose. Her son Nick conned her, terrorised her and even tried to kill her. Grandson Ashley was killed in a bike crash. Dot's been beaten, mugged and incarcerated. Some would say she was asking for it with her God-bothering self-righteousness – but surely no one deserves to be married to Jim Branning...

Lou Beale

The matriarchs' matriarch, Lou ruled with a rod of iron, constantly calling 'family meetings' to keep her clan in line, and, when she didn't get her way, taking to her bed. She'd have had you believe she was a pillar of moral perfection – and yet Lou, too, had her secrets, like a daughter born out of wedlock.

Mo Harris

Mo Senior is a very wicked old woman indeed. When we first met her she was doing a thriving trade in fencing stolen goods, and continues to have useful contacts in the East End criminal underworld. Unlike her fellow matriarchs, she makes absolutely no claim to be anything other than what she is – which is just as well, as she recently worked on a sex chat line as 'Miss Whiplash'.

Ethel Skinner

Too feeble to be a real battleaxe, Ethel was nonetheless a real troublemaker when the mood took her, spreading the most insane rumours about all and sundry. She pretended to be a scarlet woman, but poor old Ethel never really recovered from the death of her beloved husband Willy – or his little canine namesake.

Also:

- ▷ Auntie Nellie, who made life hell for Pauline and Arthur
- ▷ Doris, who nearly stole Jim from Dot
- ▷ Aunt Sal, Peggy's resilient sister, who liked the odd tipple
- ▷ Mo Butcher, Frank's interfering mother

1991

Mark comes to terms with his condition

Mark is HIV-positive

Mark's return to the Square in 1990 set ticking a time-bomb that would explode over Albert Square on Boxing Day of 1991. At first he was just his usual secretive, moody, miserable self, but after a while even Pauline began to realise that something was wrong with her son. She found mysterious helpline cards in his jeans and noticed that he was prone to have the vapours if he cut himself – but Pauline, far from being a woman of the world, failed to put two and two together and realise that Mark was, in fact, concealing his HIV status.

The truth emerged when Mark told Diane, his on/off platonic girlfriend, that he had come into contact with the virus through Gill, his girlfriend in Newcastle, who turned up briefly in Walford in the middle of the year but disappeared (for now) when she saw Mark kissing Diane. In fact, the relationship between Mark and Diane never really became serious; she was a useful confidante, but little more. She did, at least, encourage Mark to face facts and go for counselling at the Terrence Higgins Trust, where at last he found someone to whom he could pour out his heart.

By the middle of the year, Mark had reached an impasse; he felt unable to discuss the subject with his parents (and who can blame him?), but afraid to move on in case he became ill. In the end he was shamed into action by his friend Joe, a young, gay HIV-positive man who turned up in the Square, got a job at Ian Beale's Meal Machine and was promptly sacked when Ian discovered his status. (Ian subsequently went crazy with the bleach bottle in an attempt to 'disinfect' his premises.) Joe encouraged Mark to tell his parents the truth, and persuaded him of the unhealthy effects of keeping secrets.

Eventually, with further encouragement from Rachel (with whom he slept), Mark decided to drop the big one, and let it all out to Pauline and Arthur on Boxing Day. They sat in stunned silence while he scattered a few helpful leaflets around the house and fled to the countryside. When he returned, he faced cringeing terror from Pauline, hostility from Arthur – and the prospect of a very difficult New Year.

Eddie's Murder

Who killed Eddie Royle? That was the question on everyone's lips during the last few months of 1991, after the publican's lifeless carcass was found, early one morning, in the middle of the Square. The finger of suspicion pointed at Grant Mitchell, who had been spoiling for a fight with Eddie for months over Sharon, and Clyde Tavernier, who had got involved with some shady dealings relating to his boxing career. Both of them protested their innocence – but, unfortunately for Clyde, there were witnesses who had seen him bending over the body holding a bloodstained knife.

For weeks he was to be seen skulking around the Community Centre, moodily claiming that he was a victim of a racist conspiracy, much to the delight of kid brother Lloyd, who thought he was a hero. When Grant was cleared of any involvement in the crime, the police started closing in on Clyde, who hid out in Rachel and Michelle's house. Instead of explaining to the police that he had found the body, panicked, picked up the knife and then destroyed the evidence, Clyde decided to go on the run instead. Michelle stood by her man and joined him on the dash to Portsmouth with Kofi and Vicki – where they were easily picked up by the police and returned to Walford.

Fortunately for all concerned, Joe came forward to attest that he had seen Nick Cotton climbing down the drainpipe on the night of the murder. Dot extracted a confession of murder from her repentant

Eddie Royle (Michael Melia) meets his Maker

son, and Clyde was off the hook. Eddie remained well and truly dead, thus leaving the tenancy of the Vic up for grabs.

Ricky and Sam

Ever since they first laid eyes on each other, Ricky and Sam knew that they were meant to be together. They had so much in common: overbearing parents, unbearable siblings and a shared bond of stupidity (both of them were crashing academic failures, with a single biology GCSE between them). And so, naturally, Ricky proposed to Sam and, on being accepted, proceeded to tell the world on the occasion of her 16th birthday. Sam's mother, bossy

Young hearts run free: Ricky and Sam in Gretna Green

Peggy Mitchell, did all she could to crush love's young dream, but succeeded instead in driving them closer together; had she never read *Romeo and Juliet*? Ricky and Sam started sneaking off to cheap 'otels in 'Ackney, or spending nights in their camper-van 'nookiemobile' before planning their elopement to Gretna Green.

This was planned with all the efficiency you'd expect from Ricky, who not only failed to procure a wedding licence or book a registry office, but also left an RAC map of his destination hanging around the Arches, just in case anyone needed to follow them. And so began a comic chase up and down Great Britain, which finally came to a romantic conclusion when Pat agreed to assist at the marriage while the marauding Mitchells burst in to prevent the ceremony. Unfortunately for them, they'd picked the wrong ceremony; their little girl was getting married in an entirely different town.

Mr and Mrs Ricky Butcher returned to Walford with their heads held high, and even managed to persuade Peggy to come to their blessing ceremony. This turned out to be the high point of their relationship. Unable to afford their own home, they sulked around the B&B until Sam got itchy feet and started flouncing off at the drop of a hat. Once her love for Ricky was no longer illegal, she began to wonder if she'd got such a great bargain after all.

Etta and Celestine

The Taverniers didn't have an easy year. As well as having to cope with a son on the run for suspected murder, after a pregnancy scare Etta decided that she should undergo sterilisation in order not to pass on her sickle-cell gene to any future children. Celestine, a pompous pillar of righteousness, objected to the plan but, when Etta discovered that she was already pregnant, and that the child had a double dose of the gene, he was forced to reappraise his priorities and to agree, unwillingly, to a termination.

Things weren't helped by the fact that Etta was enjoying professional success; at the beginning of the year, she was promoted to the headship of the school at which she taught. Patriarchal Celestine was threatened by his wife's status, and immediately fell into the waiting arms of Yvonne, a sympathetic lady friend from church, who offered much more than tea and sympathy. The danger passed, and the marriage remained intact, but Celestine remained a self-righteous fool to the end. He drove Hattie away from home by objecting to her dress sense (and almost drove her into the arms of Ian Beale – a fate worse than death), and only seemed to come to life when he'd drunk the best part of a bottle of rum.

Michelle and Clyde

Michelle took a look in the mirror in early 1991 and realised what the viewing nation had been thinking for years – that she was looking worn out. She tried to glam herself up, to little avail, but she did at least attract the attention of Clyde Tavernier, a fellow single parent who seemed eager for friendship. Michelle moved out of her parents' house and found lodgings with Rachel, the English lecturer, who encouraged her to go back to college and introduced her to some of her posh friends. Rachel read *Spare Rib*, cooked vegetarian food and – worst of all – didn't have a telly, much to Pauline's disgust. This didn't deter Michelle, who adopted Rachel as her new best friend (Sharon called her 'a condescending bitch'). The pair became so inseparable that the Square was alive with lesbian rumours, which Michelle silenced by sleeping with Clyde.

The relationship was short-lived, and fizzled out after Clyde had been cleared of murder. Michelle had been ready to move to France with him, but thought better of it once he'd been cleared of murder. As he was by that time neither married, nor a suspected criminal, Michelle lost interest.

Disa

Dopey Disa, Diane's homeless friend, dumped her baby in Albert Square on Christmas Day 1990, but soon reappeared to become the worst mother in the history of the show – worse, even, than Punk Mary, and that's something. The baby (who was first called Billie, later Jasmine) was snatched by a man called Ken, who claimed to be Disa's uncle but turned out to be a) her stepfather and b) the father of her child, thanks to a spot of incest/rape. Ken was arrested but later bailed, leaving Disa to go berserk with a carving knife, but fortunately the villain was banged up on remand. Disa's mother turned up to claim her wayward daughter (and new granddaughter – or was she her stepdaughter?), and Disa left Walford for good.

EVERYONE TALKED ABOUT…

Mark's big bombshell

There are many ways to ruin your family's Christmas in Albert Square – serving divorce papers, for instance – but Mark Fowler still tops the league for great festive spoilers. After months of concealing his HIV status, he finally plucked up the courage to come out to Pauline and Arthur – and somehow it just had to be on Boxing Day. To a nation still lamentably uninformed about Aids, this was a revelation, and the HIV storyline remains *EastEnders*' most effective piece of issue-based drama.

Mark was never the most articulate EastEnder in the world, so this was never going to be easy…

…particularly when Arthur and Pauline gave him that special hostile, icy look with which they met most of their children's confidences

Undeterred, Mark said the words that his parents did not want to hear. Arthur was instantly hostile, which didn't help matters

Nobody could blame Mark for fleeing Walford. He returned to face the music in the New Year

Mr and Mrs Grant Mitchell tie the knot – shortly before sleeping with witnesses Michelle and Phil

Sharon and Grant

It took a while for Sharon and Grant's relationship to get off the ground; every time she got close to him, he would freak out and start shouting in his sleep. But there was something about his criminal allure that kept Sharon coming back for more, and when she saw Grant beating Eddie Royle to a pulp in a jealous rage she knew that this was the real thing. Grant confessed that he was a total psychopath and had been ever since killing a defenceless 16-year-old boy in the Falklands – by which time Sharon was pressing him to name the day.

Grant gave Sharon her heart's desire by securing the tenancy of the Queen Vic after Eddie's death, and the pair were married on Boxing Day. The audience gave it six months, maximum.

Nick's Addiction

Nick Cotton turned up again in June, begging and stealing to feed a full-blown heroin habit. At first Dot hardened her heart (he had tried to murder her the previous year), but when she discovered that her husband Charlie, Nick's father, had been killed in an accident on the M25, she decided she'd better try to be a good mother. She took Nick in, attempted to wean him off heroin and even went out to buy his drugs for him. Her 'tough love' policy led to Nick being locked in his bedroom with bars on the window. This wasn't enough, apparently, to prevent him from sneaking out at night and murdering Eddie Royle.

Also...

▶ Pete adopts a boy called Jason, a victim of parental abuse... ▶ The Mitchell brothers pass forged fivers around the Square... ▶ Eddie is visited by Eibhlin, an old flame from Ireland, and proposes marriage to her... ▶ Clyde enjoys some success in the boxing ring... ▶ Arthur gets the contract for the upkeep of the Square... ▶ Pete and Kathy's divorce comes through... ▶ Pat and Frank hit a bad patch, and Pat starts hanging around in pick-up joints...

Soft Touches

Permanently confused, sexually bungling men are a mainstay of Walford society. These poor souls exist to be trampled, disappointed and taken for a ride by any crook or schemer that crosses their path.

Arthur Fowler

As if it wasn't enough to be permanently henpecked by his wife, Arthur was always ready to fling himself into any dodgy scheme going. Incapable of holding down a job, he was always looking for easy cash to pay for weddings, funerals and the like – and so he stole and went to prison for it. A crook he may have been (and an improbable adulterer), but Arthur wasn't man enough to live the criminal life, and was constantly breaking down in the allotment shed, where it finally all got too much for him and he collapsed. He died a permanently disappointed man.

Mark Fowler

Mark used to be quite a feisty little fellow, running around with gangs and breaking his poor mother's heart. But when he returned to full-time residency in the 90s, Mark was a changed man. He was heroic when confronting the Square's prejudice over his HIV status, but thereafter he existed largely to be taken for a ride by needy, mentally unstable women like Diane, Gill, Ruth and Lisa. His death in 2004, however, united the warring Walfordians in grief.

Pete Beale

It was hard to like poor Pete Beale. He started off as such a cheery chappy, and yet, within a few years, his marriage was on

the rocks. His failure to support Kathy through her rape ordeal lost him any shred of public sympathy, and he languished in market half-life until Rose Chapman's gangster brothers disposed of him in 1993.

Lofty Holloway

Lofty was the connoisseur's choice of mugs. Thin, myopic and asthmatic, not only did he look like the sort of person that you just wanted to suffer, he was also permanently, humiliatingly at the disposal of Michelle Fowler. He unknowingly agreed to raise Den's baby as his own and to marrying Michelle (despite her standing him up at the altar). He finally left her after she aborted their baby against his will.

Ricky Butcher

Ricky suffered the misfortune of being a) quite stupid and b) one of the few attractive men in Walford. This meant that aggressive, frustrated women flung themselves at him, and he was powerless to resist. Natalie had him (twice), Sam married him, Bianca married him, and Mandy had him just for something to do. The trouble was, once these women had him, they didn't know what to do with him – and Ricky was left, as ever, looking hurt and confused.

Roy Evans

Roy existed to be cheated on, dumped, swindled and duped. He thought of himself as a decent man, and yet he got involved in every dodgy scam going, and, as we later found, had been off with another woman when his own wife died. Marriage to Pat proved to be too much for him, and he finally dropped dead – of exhaustion, more than anything.

Barry Evans

Muggishness runs in East End families, and Barry was just as much of a dupe as his father. He was conned by Vanessa for every penny he (and his father) had; later he was conned by Janine, and pushed off a cliff for his trouble. In between times he

managed to marry Natalie, but she left him for Ricky – which just proves that everything is relative.

Also:

▷ Robbie Jackson, well-intentioned drone

▷ Alan Jackson, Carol's not-too-bright husband

▷ Anthony Trueman, the meat in a Slater-girl sandwich

▷ Eddie Royle, murder victim

▷ Nigel Bates, everyone's best mate, terrible taste in shirts

▷ Geoff Barnes, much more than Michelle's tutor

▷ Ali Osman, gambling addict

▷ Gianni Di Marco, strong in the arm, thick in the head

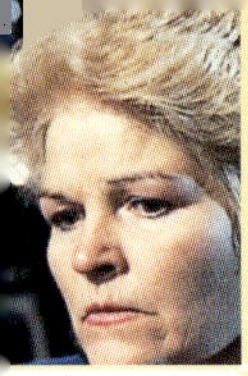

1992

Arthur with suburban sexpot Mrs Hewitt (Elizabeth Power)

Arthur and Mrs Hewitt

What ended up being dubbed the 'Bonk of the Year!' by the tabloids all started off quite innocently when a buoyant Arthur got a bit of gardening work from a lonely divorcee called Christine Hewitt. At first they merely shared a taste for horticulture, but when Pauline conveniently disappeared to New Zealand for a few months to tend her brother Kenny after a car crash, Arthur began to realise that there might be more to the fairer sex than constant nagging and drab knitwear. Before you knew it, Arthur and Mrs H were hanging around the Square together, kissing in alleyways and generally behaving like a pair of randy teenagers. Unfortunately for them, their furtive gropings were caught on camera by Jules Tavernier, the proud new owner of a video camera, and their dangerous liaison was soon the talk of the Square.

The longer Pauline stayed away, the worse things got. First of all, Pete started competing with Arthur for the lovely Christine, and when that failed to sting her sluggish lover into action, she found excuses to spend the night at 45 Albert Square. Dot spied her at the window wearing Pauline's dressing gown and before long Walford was ringing with tall tales of Arthur's sexual prowess.

In fact, however, nothing had actually happened, and Mrs Hewitt realised she was barking up the wrong tree. She declared her love by letter, and sent a photograph which Arthur, romantic fool that he was, put up in his allotment shed – a shrine to something that never was.

That should have been the end of that, but when Pauline returned from New Zealand she seemed to have become even more obnoxious as a result of her holiday, treating Arthur like a slave and getting into fights with anyone who stood still for long enough. Arthur compared his shrew of a wife with the fragrant, lovelorn Mrs Hewitt – and scarpered straight back into her arms. Pauline found out the truth, and had a confrontation with her rival, only to be told that nothing had happened, that Arthur had simply shown kindness, that he was worth ten of her, and so forth. Pauline swallowed the lot, and went home prepared to bury the hatchet – unaware that Arthur was more interested in burying himself in the ample bosom of his outer-London lady friend. Mrs Hewitt seethed with indignation, then relented just in time to bed Arthur on Christmas Eve. By the end of the year, they were planning a full-blown secret affair.

Sharon and the Mitchell Brothers

Those who gave Sharon and Grant's marriage six months were being optimistic; barely were the daffodils up in Albert Square than Mr and Mrs Mitchell were rowing. Grant wanted a baby, Sharon didn't. Grant wanted a wife who behaved like a wife; Sharon didn't. Despite her claims to the contrary,

Torn between two lovers: Sharon considers her options

Sharon stayed on the pill, and, when Grant started to get himself involved in a raid on a betting shop, found herself confiding more and more in his sympathetic brother.

And so began the affair that was to have explosive results a couple of years later with the notorious 'Sharongate' tapes. Grant did everything he could to drive his wife and brother together; he bullied Sharon, bitched at her friends and then, when he discovered that Sharon was still using contraceptives, smashed up the bar of the Vic. Shortly after that he got it into his thick head that it would be a good idea to 'torch' the Vic in order to get the insurance money, unaware of the fact that his wife was still inside. Sharon escaped with only minor injuries to her dignity, and while she recovered in hospital she began to realise that she'd married the wrong brother.

Thenceforward, the two guilty lovebirds stole kisses whenever and wherever they could, most memorably in a fuse cupboard during a power cut. The all-seeing Michelle caught them together more than once, and soon had Sharon confessing all; this was not a good secret to share, with a psychopath like Grant on the loose. Soon even Grant began to suspect that his wife might have another bloke, and threatened to kill whoever it was. Phil was forced into the uncomfortable position of mediating between his brother and his lover, but by the end of the year both he and Sharon were convinced that they were meant for each other. Neither of them, however, had quite plucked up the courage to tell Grant. That was one cat that would stay a little longer in the bag.

In sickness and in health: Mark and Gill's (Susanna Dawson) deathbed wedding

Mark and Gill

The shock of Mark's confession continued to reverberate throughout 1992, although it remained, for the time being, a secret shared only by the immediate family. Michelle guessed the truth of the situation, and was understandably hurt that her brother hadn't confided in her; so thenceforth she would be his staunchest ally.

Things weren't good at home; Arthur had taken to ripping up Mark's helpful leaflets and bleaching the cutlery that his son had eaten with. This thrust Mark back into the arms of his girlfriend Gill, who moved down to London and started to become seriously ill. Her deterioration was rapid; she was diagnosed with non-Hodgkin's lymphoma and was placed in a hospice. Mark realised that he was truly in love with her, which was not surprising considering that the other women in his life at this time were Michelle's unbearable landlady Rachel and Mandy the poisonous teenager.

Mark and Gill memorably tied the knot in June, and managed one night of their honeymoon in a hotel before Gill was readmitted to the hospice to die. Mark spent the rest of the year in shock, more often drunk than not, and the HIV storyline was put on the back burner.

Mandy

There have been very few *EastEnders* characters as entirely loathsome as Mandy Salter. She arrived in Walford on Pat's coat tails; she was the daughter of Lorraine, a dodgy friend of Pat's, and she soon established herself as the serpent in an East End Eden. First of all she tried to blackmail Ian into giving her a job; she'd seen him picking up prostitutes, and thought that would be a good first step on the career ladder. She tried to come between Hattie and Steve, she stole money from Pete's stall, and she became obsessed with Mark, stealing his dead wife's diary and dressing up in her clothes. Amazingly, nobody bashed her head in with a brick; instead, just about everyone in the Square allowed her to live with them at one time or another before she ended the year homeless.

Ian and Cindy

Ian did not take Cindy's desertion well. He took it out on the world by becoming a power-crazed sadist with profound sexual problems, not to mention an infestation of cockroaches at the Meal Machine. He started picking up Cindy-lookalike prostitutes, and hiring 'escorts' to pretend to be his girlfriend. When he finally did persuade a real live woman to sleep with him, he ended the relationship by ruining her life and publicly calling her a slut. But beneath all this macho behaviour, Ian was just a hurting little boy – at least, that's what Kathy believed – who was missing his missus.

He remedied this situation by stalking Cindy, having seemingly forgotten that only a few months ago he was thinking of murdering her. She turned up in a grotty flat, abandoned by Wicksy who had flown the coop after only six months of domestic bliss, struggling to bring up Steven as a single mother on a low income. Ian took control of the situation, throwing money around, smothering Cindy in champagne and red roses and luring her back to Walford for Christmas for a grand reconciliation. Cindy didn't resist – she couldn't afford to – but even she realised that Ian was acting a bit creepy.

Pat and Frank

The Butchers were in deep financial trouble, owing tens of thousands of pounds to the taxman, and were forced to sell the B&B in order to keep their heads above water. Pat, however, discovered a hitherto unsuspected business flair, and started a taxi service, PatCabs, that started to make some real money by the end of the year. All seemed well until, five miles an hour and two gin and tonics over the limit, she knocked down a teenage girl on Christmas Eve. After a dreadful week, she learned that the girl had never awoken from her coma, and died on New Year's Eve. It was the start of a long, dark night of the soul for Pat Butcher.

Pat is breathalysed by a member of the Walford Constabulary

EVERYONE TALKED ABOUT…

Grant's a firestarter, a twisted firestarter

The residents of Albert Square are a bunch of pyromaniacs, quite frankly, and whenever they're in a tight spot they're apt to reach for the matches. Both the Mitchell brothers were enthusiastic arsonists, but Grant took the biscuit in 1992 by nearly burning his wife to death as well as torching his place of business, just to get the insurance.

'I'm sorry, we're not taking any party bookings at the pub tonight.' Grant takes care of a bit of business

The flames get a grip at a theoretically empty Vic

There's nothing the locals like more than a nice bonfire. A crowd gathers in Albert Square

Grant gives us his best 'shocked horror' expression as he realises that his wife is about to combust

Also...

▶ Sam does a topless modelling shoot, much to Ricky's disgust... ▶ Willmott-Brown reappears in the Square and tries to get together with Kathy, only to be driven out of Walford again... ▶ Pete attempts to adopt a strange boy called Jason, a victim of parental abuse... ▶ Michelle and Clyde's relationship fizzles out by the end of the year... ▶ Celestine and Etta move to Norwich with Lloyd... ▶ Arthur's garden gnome Norman is kidnapped... ▶ Richard 'Tricky Dicky' Cole, the market manager, has affairs with Rachel and Kathy... ▶ Nigel moves in as Dot's lodger... ▶ Little Willy, Ethel's beloved pug, meets his maker...

Market lothario Richard "Tricky Dicky" Cole (Ian Reddington)

Diamond Geezers

They're a little bit wide, a little bit dodgy, but they've got hearts of gold and we'd be lost without them.

Alfie Moon

Okay, so he got the tenancy of the Vic under false pretences. Okay, so he cleared out the till and did a moonlighter (before leaving the takings on Peggy's doorstep). Okay, so he's done time for fraud. But Alfie Moon is really, truly a nice man who has only ever ripped other people off to support his kid brother Spencer and his barmy Nana. His heart of gold became apparent the moment he met Kat Slater, who brought out the best in him. His happiness was short-lived, though, and jealousy soon destroyed his marriage. Alfie ended 2004 as he arrived in 2002, penniless and single.

Billy Mitchell

Billy wasn't always a nice man. In fact, he used to be utterly revolting. He regularly beat his nephew Jamie to a pulp, he lied, cheated and sneaked on anyone that moved. But Little Mo changed all that. Billy suddenly became a decent, upstanding man – and we realised that all that violence and crime was just a cry for help after a sad, abused childhood. Billy will never be a hero, but as men in Walford go, he's not bad, although he was unable to accept Little Mo's baby as his own.

Colin Russell

As the first of Walford's spectacularly few gay characters, Colin had a lot to put up with. He was vilified by all and sundry, he was blackmailed by Nick Cotton, and he even had to go out with Barry, the podgy barrow boy. But Colin bore it all with a saintly patience, and always had a sympathetic ear for his neighbours' problems. How they must miss him.

Charlie Slater

Considering what he has to put up with – a criminal mother-in-law, four variously demented daughters, a granddaughter who is also his niece and a child-molesting incestuous brother – Charlie ain't half bad. True, he's a bit handy with his fists, but you would be in his shoes. After taking a shine to Peggy – and being promptly rebuffed – the man deserves a break.

Rod Norman

Rod the Roadie was a one-man social services for the lost girls of Walford in the early days of *EastEnders*. He managed to get Punk Mary off the game, and helped her to keep her child. He took pity on druggie Donna when everyone else would have crossed the road to avoid her. Finally he picked up, and took off, with Nick Cotton's discarded 'wife' Hazel.

Garry Hobbs

Some people would put Garry in the 'mug' category, but there's actually something rather heroic about him. He's put up with Lynne's erratic moodswings, and has fought off her randy sister Kat; why, he's even been obliged to service Slater sister Belinda.
When Laura named him as the father of her baby, he stuck by her – which may not be very bright, but at least has the ring of nobility about it.

Also:

- ▷ Jim Branning, permanent barprop
- ▷ Jules Tavernier, brought a twinkle to the old girls' eyes
- ▷ Alex Healy, had to be nice – he was a vicar
- ▷ Jeff Healy, Pauline's rejected boyfriend
- ▷ Patrick Trueman, never says no to a drink
- ▷ Derek Harkinson, Pauline's platonic partner

The Big Issues

One of the criticisms most frequently levelled at *EastEnders* is that it is 'miserable' or 'depressing'. This, however, doesn't stop people from tuning in in their millions, so it must be assumed that, for whatever reason, audiences enjoy those particular qualities of the drama.

Ever since it began in 1985, *EastEnders* has striven to incorporate into the fabric of a family-based soap opera some of the most contentious issues of its time. '*EastEnders* was born out of a desire to reflect the changes that were happening in society in the mid 80s,' says Mal Young, the BBC's controller of drama series from 1997 to 2004. 'It's continued to mirror those changes for 20 years. It's a narrative that runs in parallel to our own lives, and as long as it continues to do so it will remain in rude health.'

Unplanned pregnancies, often terminated, have formed the backbone of many a storyline, as have adultery, infidelity, homosexuality and many other variations on a theme of sex. Crime, too, has reared its ugly head in many guises: murder, rape, assault,

VALUE ASSURED
FRANK'S
"Come & have a

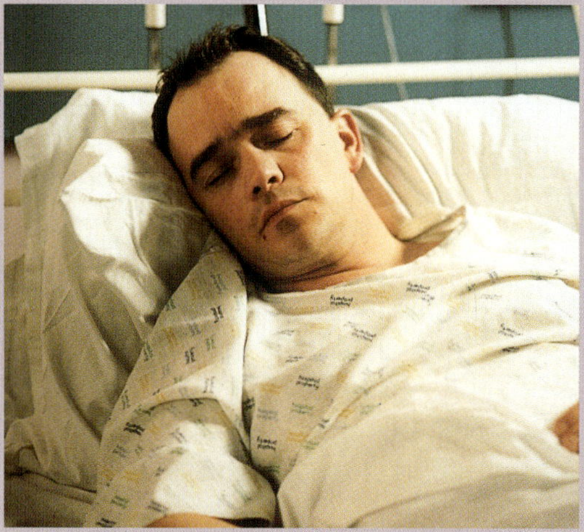

abuse, theft, arson, drug-dealing, fraud, you name it. Health issues have fuelled some of *EastEnders*' most vivid storylines, from Mark's HIV diagnosis through Mo's Alzheimer's disease to Peggy's breast cancer and Sam's breast cancer scare.

'What soaps can do is to shed light on issues that are happening all around us,' says Young. '*EastEnders* is not led by issues; that's not the way good drama should be. It happened on *Brookside* in later years, and we ended up with the issues coming first, with a result that the show was very earnest and nobody cared about the characters. But *EastEnders* looks at what's really going on in the world, and addresses those things in a forthright way. I don't think it leads public opinion; it's made by programme makers, not politicians. If they had all the answers, they'd be running the country, not making drama. But the programme does have a responsibility to raise awareness about things. Drama has always done that; it's brought things out of the shadows and into the light. *EastEnders* can do that in an extremely effective way. The team has often heard from parents who say that it has allowed them to tackle things with their children, particularly in the areas of sex and drugs, that they would have found it very difficult to address without the context of *EastEnders*.'

While Young and the show's team are reluctant to blow the trumpet for *EastEnders* as a leader of public opinion, there's no doubt that the show has done much to blow away the cobwebs of prejudice that were a lot thicker in 1985 than they are in 2005. When Colin and Barry enjoyed their first on-screen kiss in 1986, there were howls of protest from the right-wing papers – and huge sighs of relief from gay viewers who, before that time, had never been represented in mass-audience mainstream TV except as caricatures. Similarly, Mark's Aids storyline (1991) was condemned as being too much for a 7.30pm timeslot – and yet it did more than any

The Ferreiras – Dan, Ash, Ronny, Kareena and Adi

number of government campaigns to ram home some basic facts about HIV infection and to address (through Dot and Peggy) the ignorance and prejudice faced by people with Aids.

The same is true of its treatment of other intense personal issues. Michelle's pregnancy by Den, and Sonia's pregnancy by Martin, explored areas of experience that were common to thousands of viewers. When storylines touched on even more painful and contentious issues – Kathy's rape by Willmott-Brown, for instance, or the domestic violence and sexual abuse inflicted on Little Mo by Trevor – *EastEnders* was deluged with letters from grateful viewers who felt that their own sufferings had been assuaged or vindicated by the show.

Looking back on 20 years' worth of stories, it's possible to trace the evolution of attitudes towards certain social issues that has been pinpointed by major *EastEnders* storylines. When Michelle was carrying Den's child, what shocked audiences most was the age difference – teenage pregnancy, while no longer rare, was still a matter for raised eyebrows. Michelle was almost ostracised by her shocked family, and faced her predicament alone. When Sonia unexpectedly went into labour with Martin's baby 17 years later, everyone rallied round to support her. Accidental teenage pregnancy was no longer a disgrace, but a misfortune that could be visited on anyone.

EastEnders has also tried hard, over the decades, to reflect the increasingly diverse society in which we live. The integration of different racial groups hasn't always been the show's strongest suit, and for some reason the writers have always found it hard to come up with good, universal storylines for characters of African or Asian origin. But even that's changing. The Square's first Asian residents, Saeed and Naima Jeffery, kept a corner shop and had an arranged marriage; so far, so stereotypical. Compare the Ferreiras, who arrived in 2003 with an arsenal of storylines involving adultery, drug-dealing, father-son romantic rivalry and that old *EastEnders* chestnut, mysterious paternity. Their ethnicity was an important part of the family's overall character, but it was not their defining characteristic.

The turning point in the depiction of non-white characters was, perhaps, the Tavernier family. They started off in 1990 with stock storylines about strict church morality and sickle-cell anaemia. By the time they left, what everyone chiefly remembered was oldest son Clyde's affair with Michelle (yes, her again) – one of the very first high-profile mixed-race relationships on TV.

Now, as *EastEnders* moves into its third decade, more effort than ever is made to ensure that the show gives an accurate reflection of the world it represents. An annual 'MOT health check' draws on the opinions of thousands of viewers gathered by an independent research company – and the producers know that punches will not be pulled. 'They will tell you in no uncertain terms if the programme has failed them,' says Mal Young. 'They will also surprise you by the things they like. The show can't rest on its laurels; it has to keep on evolving, because society itself evolves. If it got stuck in a certain style, it would die out. I've actually been pleased when people have told me that the show isn't what it used to be; that's the whole point. It changes all the time, while retaining certain key features that make it what it is. When you see old episodes on satellite TV, they should look dated. It's all about reflecting change. As far as I'm concerned, *EastEnders* is only as good as last night's episode.'

Young is the first to admit that *EastEnders* has sometimes got it wrong. 'When we did our research a couple of years ago, a lot of people were complaining that the show was too depressing. Now that's a criticism the programme is used to, and sometimes it's just a reaction to the realism of the storylines. But on this occasion it was in response to a very dark, violent period on the show, around the time of Grant's departure and Phil's descent into crime. We felt that we were reflecting a growth in violent crime – but the viewers felt that the show had lost a lot of its warmth. There's a balance to be struck there. *EastEnders* will never fight shy of the darker side of life, but it has to be done with warmth and humour as well. I don't mean it's going to turn into a sitcom; I just think that you can balance the grim stuff better.'

There are also concerns surrounding the content of a programme that goes out in the early evening and on Sunday afternoons. 'I don't need reminding that *EastEnders* has to be suitable for an unsupervised child to watch,' says Young, 'because I have a seven-year-old daughter of my own. The show is

Being in a mixed-race relationship with Michelle was the least of Clyde's worries

Janine (Charlie Brooks) succumbs to drugs and prostitution

very aware of the pre-watershed time slot, but that doesn't mean it waters down the drama. It won't show certain things, and it's careful with the language, but it'll still take viewers to the heart of difficult issues. When Janine went on the game to finance her cocaine habit, there were a lot of raised eyebrows – but I think we handled that storyline in a sensitive way. The drama was challenging, but it wasn't offensive. Little children wouldn't have understood it, but, let's face it, most kids know what these things are about these days. It's the common currency of the playground. TV has certainly contributed to that awareness, but you can't blame TV for the existence of those issues in the first place. Whatever's going on in society, children will pick up on it.'

EastEnders has lasted for 20 years because it has a strong sense of its own style: the clothes, the accents and the storylines are all distinctively, recognisably Albert Square. And that distinctiveness is at the heart of the strategy for the next 20 years. 'There's so much choice in the TV market these days that it has to refine its act more and more,' says Young. 'It's no longer enough to assume that people will automatically tune into BBC1 in the evening; there's an ever-increasing number of alternatives. It has to be very clear about what it's delivering, and the programme makers have to make sure that the audience understands and likes what they're doing. *EastEnders* has to remain different and distinctive from the other soaps. That's not because it's competing with *Coronation Street* or *Emmerdale* – I think that's a myth, because people watch whatever they want to watch. It's just that they don't want soap to become a generic mush of all the same things. It has to stay true to its roots and its individuality.'

And what exactly defines *EastEnders* as compared, say, to *Coronation Street*? 'Underneath everything the show does, there's a very strong sense of place,' says the show's former executive producer, Louise Berridge. 'The East End spirit has its roots in the Blitz. It's about survival against the odds, whatever threats come from outside. The physical nature of the East End has changed a lot, even since the show started: the buildings, the businesses and even the accents are different now. But I think the spirit is still there. It's a very inward-looking society. You distrust and exclude outsiders, you keep your own secrets, you solve your own problems and you don't involve the police unless you absolutely have to. You look after your family first. That's the identity of *EastEnders*. It's not just about a bunch of characters who happen to live in the same square. They're defined by a shared ethos. The same could be said of *Coronation Street*, where people are much more sociable and outward-looking and welcoming. In *EastEnders* you're dealing with that tradition of poverty, of survival at any cost – and it's been shrunk down to one little Square. It's a world in miniature. That kind of inwardness and secrecy is a horrible thing to live with, but it makes for great drama, and as long as they stick to that they'll never be short of gripping storylines.'

Mark's funeral: the final curtain on one of EastEnders*' most controversial storylines*

Welcome to Walford

The birth of a new baby should always be a joyful occasion – but that's not always the case around Albert Square. Relive 20 years of unplanned pregnancies, phantom fathers and adoption dramas.

Pauline's late-life pregnancy, 1985

Nobody, least of all Pauline, expected **Martin** to come along when he did. But thankfully there was no doubt as to who was the father: Pauline hadn't strayed from Arthur's bed in all those long years of marriage.

Michelle's mystery baby, 1985

One of the first great *EastEnders* scandals concerned the paternity of Michelle's baby **Vicki**, born in 1986. For a long time she concealed the fact that this was the result of a single night of passion with Den, her best friend's Dad.

Who is Simon's father? 1986

You don't have to be a new-born baby to be at the centre of a pregnancy scandal. When **Simon Wicks** returned to Walford in 1985, Pat immediately claimed that he was not, after all, Pete Beale's son, as he had always believed. Suspicion fell on brother Kenny – but it turned out, eventually, that Brian Wicks was to blame.

Cindy's big surprise, 1989

When Cindy gave birth to **Steven**, it was reasonable to assume that Ian (her husband at the time) was the father. Anyone with a head for sums could see that didn't add up, however – so Cindy just said Steven was premature. The fact was, of course, that he wasn't Ian's at all, but Simon's.

Sharon finds her mother, 1990

Let down by her warring adoptive parents, **Sharon** understandably decided to find her birth mother after they had gone. It was a long quest before she was united with Carol – only to realise that, despite their faults, Den and Angie were the people who raised her and she had to accept it.

Disa's Christmas bundle, 1990

Homeless Disa O'Brien arrived in Albert Square heavily pregnant, and, with immaculate timing, gave birth to baby **Billie** in a derelict house on Christmas Day, and promptly tried to give her away. It turned out that Billie (later renamed Jasmine) was the offspring of Disa's abusive stepfather.

Double trouble for Ian and Cindy, 1993

Despite the ups and downs of their marriage, Ian and Cindy did manage to have two legitimate children – twins **Lucy and Peter** – during one of her rare stays in the marital home.

Grant's mystery son, 1995

Grant Mitchell always wanted to be a father – but, ironically, he actually had a son in 1996, the result of an ill-advised encounter with Michelle, who promptly fled to America carrying his child. This turned out to be the mysterious **Mark Junior**, whom we have never since seen. When Sharon left earlier in the same year, she too was pregnant by Grant – but had a termination.

Kathy's concealed pregnancy, 1995

When Kathy got pregnant by Phil, all should have been well – but Kathy didn't discover she was pregnant for over three months and then waited a further three weeks for test results before telling him. Finally, when she confessed, he was delighted and baby **Ben** was born in 1996. His parents' marriage was on the rocks by the end of the year.

Who is Courtney's Dad? 1996

Tiffany slept with Grant and Tony within days of each other, so when she fell pregnant there was naturally some confusion as to paternity. Grant was overjoyed when baby **Courtney** appeared, finally making him officially a father – and then went through hell till a blood test confirmed that he, not Tony, had done the deed.

Lou's illegitimate daughter, 1997

Who would have thought it: Lou Beale had a daughter outside wedlock, and gave it up for adoption. It turned out that Irish **Maggie** was in fact Pauline's full sister.

Is Gianni a Di Marco? 1998

Doubt was cast on the paternity of **Gianni** when his mother, Rosa, revealed that she'd been having an affair with George Palmer around the time of his conception. This didn't half put the mockers on Gianni's burgeoning affair with Annie Palmer – who suddenly could have been his half-sister.

Sonia's big surprise, 2000

Being a responsible girl, Sonia took a pregnancy test after her drunken night of passion with Martin Fowler. It was negative. Nine months later, a romantic meal with Jamie was ruined when extreme tummy ache turned out, in fact, to herald the arrival of little **Chloe** on the living room floor, assisted by Mo, who was used to that sort of thing.

Tug-of-love Louise, 2001

Lisa was convinced that fatherhood would tame Phil Mitchell, and so, after a false start (her first pregnancy miscarried), she gave birth to **Louise**. Far from saving her parents' relationship, however, Louise became the prize in a vicious game of pass the parcel, being regularly snatched by mother and father for the first few years of her life. To add to this mess, at one point Mark Fowler stepped in and told anyone who'd listen that he, not Phil, was the father.

A near miss for Jack, 2002

Natalie got a terrible case of cold feet when she discovered that her marriage to Barry was about to result in parenthood. Fearing a lifetime of drudgery, she nearly terminated the pregnancy – but then, luckily for her son **Jack**, changed her mind at the last moment.

Zoe's sister is actually her mother, 2001

Kat blurted out the truth about her relationship with **Zoe** during an argument, and later revealed the grisly fact that the father was none other than her own Uncle Harry. All hell was let loose, Zoe ran away, Harry dropped dead and mother and daughter were finally reconciled.

The further adventures of Chloe, 2002

Not content with having arrived unannounced on the living room floor, little **Chloe** went on to star in her very own adoption and kidnapping drama, as Sonia snatched her back from her new parents, who had renamed her Rebecca.

Laura's miraculous conception, 2002

Nobody was more surprised than Ian when his wife, Laura, became pregnant after he had had a vasectomy. Ian forced her to admit that this was the result of a one-night stand with Garry, who stuck around to act as a father to **Bobby** (named after Bobby Moore). When Laura died, however, Ian discovered that he was actually Bobby's father.

Dirty Den Junior, 2003

Den Watts had no idea that an idle dalliance with his mate's daughter Paula Rickman had resulted in the birth of a son, **Dennis**. It took the sleuthing skills of Vicki and Sharon to track him down and to unite him with the father he had never known, but whom he so much resembled.

Demi Miller, schoolgirl mother, 2004

The extremely trashy Miller family were proud to include among their ranks Walford's youngest-ever mother, Demi, who gave birth at the tender age of 13. And the father? An equally charming teenager, Leo.

1993

Arthur and Mrs Hewitt

Arthur's adulterous affair with Christine Hewitt turned from comedy to tragedy in 1993. While he ran between her and Pauline like a headless chicken, Mrs H became more and more needy and manipulative, cooking up absurd lies like a fake burglary in order to lure Arthur round for a quickie, then hitting the bottle if he refused to play ball. This left Arthur, never the strongest personality at the best of times, little more than a nervous wreck. Fortunately for him, Pauline wasn't as perceptive as she liked to think, and it took her a mighty long time to twig that her dependable doormat of a husband was up to something.

Besides which, Pauline had distractions of her own in the unlikely shape of Danny Taurus, an old school friend who returned to Walford as a successful club singer. He whisked Pauline off her feet, and started taking her out for dinner while Arthur was away tending Mrs H's garden. At first Pauline thought this was a bit of harmless fun, and recompense for her husband's neglect – but when Danny declared undying love, she sent him packing.

This was enough to persuade Pauline that what she really needed was a few days' leave in Leigh-on-Sea, the family's traditional bolthole. While the cat was away, mousey Arthur played the fool, snogging Mrs H in the bistro and generally behaving so indiscreetly that the all-seeing Kathy noticed something was up and extracted a confession from a tearful Christine. It was crunch time; the errant Mr Hewitt was back on the scene, forcing his wife to choose between Arthur and him. Mrs H cracked under the pressure, and for a short while *EastEnders* turned into *Fatal Attraction*, as she stalked Arthur around the Square, drunkenly declaring love and buying inappropriate gifts for Martin.

Pauline came back from Leigh-on-Sea and finally realised that her husband had been deceiving her for several months. When Arthur confessed all, Pauline responded in the time-honoured way, by lobbing the contents of her kitchen at his head. Arthur was persuaded to lie low for a while, and ended up living in a nearby dosshouse, spending his days hanging round the Square like a bad smell. Mrs Hewitt was given her marching orders, and disappeared to face a lonely future, divorced by her husband and ditched by her lover. Arthur eventually wormed his way back into Pauline's affections, and they ended the year more or less reconciled under the greater shadow cast by Pete's death.

Aidan and Mandy

Such was the power of Mandy Salter that she could transform a wholesome, football-playing, Irish boy like Aidan into a drug-addled, suicidal wreck in less than a year. Aidan appeared in the Square as an unlikely protégé of Arthur's, who managed to take an interest in the local football team in between

Aidan (Sean Maguire) before Mandy got her claws into him

adulteries. He took Aidan under his wing, and adopted him as a surrogate son, much to Pauline's consternation and the viewing public's confusion. Aidan was a likeable lad, prone to occasional bouts of naked sleepwalking in Albert Square, but he was easily led – and when Mandy got her hands on him, he kissed his footballing career goodbye.

Mandy got him drunk on tequila, and in a subsequent fall he injured his leg so badly that he could never play again. Then she lured him into club culture – this was at the height of the rave era, when any soap character who went within five miles of a disco immediately turned into a slavering drug addict. Predictably, Aidan tasted the forbidden fruit, and passed out in an Ecstasy-induced coma. After that he attempted to escape back to Ireland, but tenacious Mandy followed him and dragged him back to the Square.

The young lovers returned in the summer, and quickly established themselves as Walford's most hated residents. They broke into Pete's empty flat and started squatting. Mandy got a job cleaning Dr Legg's surgery, and repaid him by stealing prescription pads and attempting to flog them to drug dealers. Aidan was reduced to begging from his neighbours, while Mandy followed in her mother's footsteps with a little casual prostitution in King's Cross. This career path was closed to her when the other girls beat her up; even prostitutes hated Mandy Salter.

The final straw came when Mandy was indirectly responsible for the death of Roly; she took him out for a walk, and he was hit by a car. Aidan got ill, was disowned by his parents and decided to end it all by flinging himself off a tower block on Christmas Day. Mandy turned up just in time, and for some reason the sight of her made him change his mind; most of us, faced with a similar prospect, would have jumped. However, he couldn't bear the thought of another year with Mandy, and he left her before New Year. She saw in 1994 huddled and sobbing on the Fowlers' couch.

Ian and Cindy's double baby joy

Cindy and Ian

After their cosy Christmas reunion, Cindy and Ian decided that they might be able to put the past behind them and start again as a family. Kathy, however, had other ideas, and accused Cindy of being a gold digger, which was enough to make her pack her bags and leave. When Ian discovered that his own mother had driven his beloved away, he went in hot pursuit, finally tracking Cindy down in a squalid B&B where she owed rent. He persuaded her to come home with him – and Cindy, who had been ditched by Simon six months earlier, had little choice but to accept. Back in the Square, she had one of her regular stand-offs with her mother-in-law, warning Kathy that unless she was nice to her, she'd take Steven and leave for good.

Needless to say, things went badly from this point on. Cindy attracted the attentions of the hideous Richard 'Tricky Dicky' Cole, who wouldn't take no for an answer and did everything he could to cause trouble between Cindy and Ian. He managed to get Ian's Meal Machine shut down by the environmental health officers, and later, when Cindy got pregnant, told anyone who would listen that he was the father, despite the fact that they hadn't actually had sex. Kathy, and even Ian, were ready to believe the worst, but truth finally prevailed, and there was general rejoicing when Cindy was delivered of twins.

Michelle and Vicki

1993 was yet another bad year for Michelle Fowler, a woman tailor-made for misery. It wasn't enough that she was a single mother who had lost the man she loved in the local canal, had an HIV-positive brother and an adulterous father. No: Michelle also had to attract the attentions of a crazed stalker and a loopy kidnapper.

Jack, the student with whom she'd foolishly dallied in 1992, turned up in Albert Square seemingly believing that he and Michelle were meant for each other. He convinced Pauline that he was her daughter's boyfriend, then stole Michelle's unwashed knickers from the laundry basket, which ranks as one of *EastEnders*' strangest-ever courtship rituals. After that, he just got weirder, injuring himself in order to get Michelle's sympathy, picking fights with Clyde in the pub and making vaguely threatening phonecalls. Finally Michelle found an unlikely ally in Phil Mitchell, who helped her to track down Jack's parents and to extract a confession that their son had form for this sort of thing. Jack broke down and admitted everything, and then obligingly disappeared.

That's not before he'd been the prime susect in the Vicki Kidnap Drama that rocked the Square over the summer. Michelle was a little late picking Vicki up from school one day – and turned up only to discover that the child had already been taken. A national police operation eventually found Vicki in the clutches of a mad old woman called Audrey Whittingham, who just liked the look of her and decided to take her home. Michelle failed to see the funny side of this and started throwing all of Vicki's clothes in the bin, believing, perhaps with some justification, that she was not such a good mother. After all this, Michelle needed a holiday, and so went to Amsterdam with her brother and some minor characters, only to be used as a drugs mule on the way home. It could only happen to Michelle Fowler…

Sharon challenges Grant to a staring match

Sharon and the Mitchell Brothers

Sharon swanned off to spend some time with her mother at the beginning of the year – after marrying one Mitchell brother, and having an affair with the other, the poor girl must have been exhausted. When she returned in the summer, she attempted to wrest control of the Queen Vic back from her ne'er-do-well husband, who responded by beating her up and leaving her sobbing on the kitchen floor. Sharon bravely hid her bruises beneath thicker-than-usual make-up, but that didn't fool Michelle or Phil, both of whom were spoiling for a fight with Grant.

Grant got rapidly worse, smacking Sharon around, calling her a tart in public and throwing money at her, which was the final straw. Michelle stood up to the big ape, and threatened him with the police, who duly arrived in the middle of a punch-up and carted Grant off to prison. With hubby out the way, Sharon saw no obstacle to replacing him with her brother-in-law, and began sleeping with Phil on a regular basis. Like all tragic lovers, however, they were tormented by feelings of guilt, and each resolved on a weekly basis to make a clean breast of it to Grant and start a new life together. This they never managed to do, and when Grant came out of prison, broken and remorseful, the web of lies got even thicker. Sharon took pity on her vulnerable husband, who displayed signs of having become a 90s New Man; at one point he was actually seen with an iron in his hand, and it wasn't being used as a weapon at the time. Phil watched, helplessly, as Grant and Sharon kissed and made up.

For Phil, the options were clear. He instantly met and married a random Romanian refugee called Nadia, then started having an affair with Kathy during a trip to Paris. Sharon and Grant, meanwhile, ended the year in the nearest they ever got to marital bliss.

Pete and Rose

Miraculously, Pete Beale found a woman who actually liked him. Rose Chapman was another old Walfordian whom Pete met at a Danny Taurus gig, and the two of them started a little romance. Things were going well until Rose revealed that she was a) married, and that b) her husband was a psychotic gangster called Alfie Chapman. Alfie was currently detained at Her Majesty's pleasure, but the rest of the equally crazy Chapman family warned Pete that he'd better leave Rose alone…or else.

When Rose was beaten up by Alfie's caring brothers, some spark of chivalry stirred in Pete, and he rushed to the hospital, abducted his lady love and escaped through a window to start a new life in destinations unknown. Sister Pauline was distraught at her twin's disappearance, and, when she heard that Alfie Chapman had died in prison, advertised for his return. Pete replied, and the residents of Walford planned a party to celebrate his new freedom. Unfortunately for Pauline, the police arrived

EVERYONE TALKED ABOUT…

Arthur's come-uppance

We'd all known for months that Amorous Arthur was carrying on with Mrs Hewitt, but it was news to Pauline. When he finally decided to make a clean breast of it, she belaboured him with the pots and pans while a nation cheered. We don't condone violence of any kind, of course – but if anyone deserved a smart whack round the head with a frying pan, it was Arthur Fowler. It failed to knock any sense into him, but fortunately Pauline was quick to forgive.

Arthur demonstrates the finer points of his seduction technique while Pauline looks around for a weapon

Will Pauline dissolve into tears? Has Arthur got away with it?

Has he heck. Pauline tries out a new recipe – battered sod

Arthur retires, hurt, to the relative safety of the living room. Mind you, those picture frames could give you a nasty knock

Another one bites the dust: Pete's sparsely attended funeral

with the news that Pete and Rose had been killed by a hit-and-run driver – paid for by the Chapman family. And that was the end of Pete Beale.

Nigel Bates (Paul Bradley) and Debbie (Nicola Duffett)

Also...

▶ Pat serves six months in prison for killing Stephanie in a driving accident… ▶ Janine returns to live with Pat and Frank… ▶ Hattie and Steve's marriage plans go awry, and he leaves her pregnant and alone… ▶ Nick gets off at the trial for Eddie's murder, despite Dot testifying against him… ▶ Sam has an affair with Clive, then leaves Ricky to work on the cruise ships… ▶ Sanjay and his pregnant wife Gita turn up in the Square, to be joined later by her evil sister Meena… ▶ Nigel meets a woman called Debbie, with whom he begins a tormented on/off relationship… ▶ Mark has an affair of sorts with Michelle's flatmate, Shelley… ▶ Dot leaves the Square to live with Nick, Zoe and her grandson Ashley… ▶ Grant and Nigel buy a greyhound… ▶ Frank and Pat find Diane living in Paris, eight months pregnant… ▶ The Jackson family – Carol, Alan, Bianca, Robbie, Sonia and Billy – arrive in the Square, and Bianca makes a beeline for Ricky… ▶ Big Ron has a heart attack and dies...

1994

The Vic Siege

There was only one story that really mattered in 1994 – Sharongate. But in order to understand that, it's necessary to go back to some of the lesser developments in Albert Square that laid the groundwork for that most dramatic of denouements.

The year didn't start well for Mr and Mrs Grant Mitchell. He arrived home at the Vic one day with a dodgy-looking old army mate; every time one of Grant's army mates turned up in Walford, there was always trouble. This time, however, it was trouble on a grand scale. Dougie Briggs had 'psycho' written all over him, and before you knew it he was helping himself from the bar and hanging around watching Sharon in her nightie. As if that wasn't bad enough, he persuaded Grant to help him out with a raid on a supermarket, promising vast financial returns for just a little bit of business with a sawn-off shotgun.

Grant started to get cold feet about the job, and after a little digging discovered that his house guest had a little matter of a conviction for rape and murder hanging over his head. Just as Grant learned this, Sharon was innocently cashing up at the Vic, while Dougie closed in on her, hellbent on assault. After a confused battle, during which Grant was knocked unconscious, Michelle managed to get in the way of a stray bullet and ended up in a pool of blood on the Vic carpet. There was something about that carpet; Michelle just couldn't keep away from it.

Implausibly, everyone tried to cover up what had happened, rather than ringing the police and saying, 'There's a madman with a sawn-off shotgun on the loose.' While Michelle recovered in hospital, Sharon cowered in the Vic with Vicki, in the full knowledge that Dougie could be back any minute. Fortunately for all concerned, the police got to Dougie before he got to the Vic – but when Michelle discovered what peril her daughter had been in, she began to think that life in Walford wasn't all it was cracked up to be.

Sharon almost cracked under the stress, Michelle plunged into depression and even Vicki started wetting the bed. Little did they know that this was to be one of the lighter moments of their year.

Phil gets handy with the petrol

Frank and the Car Lot

Frank Butcher never had much of a head for figures, and at the beginning of the year he decided that the only way to pull himself out of his financial muddle was to burn down the car lot and claim the insurance. He had little trouble talking Phil Mitchell into striking the match, and the place went up a treat, thanks to several full tanks of petrol on the forecourt. Little did Phil and Frank know, however, that a young homeless man was sleeping rough in one of the cars, and was burned to death.

Frank was arrested on suspicion of manslaughter but later released; some doubt remained, however, as to whether or not he had conspired to defraud his insurance company. As the loss adjusters moved in, Frank claimed that his business accounts had conveniently gone up in smoke – only to find that conscientious Pat, his wife and book keeper, had handed them over to the investigating agent. The pressure became too much for Frank, who never could stand the heat, and he was last seen wandering off down Bridge Street without his wallet, keys or address book.

Frank's disappearance threw Pat into a loop. At first she assumed he'd been murdered; later, when no body showed up, she concluded that he must be holed up in Clacton, and went tearing off there to find him. Finally, however, she learned the truth: he'd simply run away. The messenger was Diane, making a brief visit from France, who had heard from her errant father and returned to Walford only to tell Pat that he wasn't coming back.

Pat could take a lot, but Frank's desertion hit her hard. She started stealing from her cleaning job in Tobago Towers, and when that wasn't enough she dipped her fingers in the till and even borrowed money from loan shark Ian Beale. She finally broke down when Sharon found her stealing from her purse. Sharon heroically bailed Pat out financially and helped her start a new life in Walford – but that was the last we saw of the old, carefree Pat. From that time hence, she was a changed woman.

Kathy and Phil

Kathy and Phil split up so often in 1994 that even regular viewers found it hard to remember the status of their relationship from one day to the next. The crunch came, however, when he confessed to Kathy his role in the car lot fire, who then decided that she couldn't love a man with such pyromaniac tendencies and went to stay with her brother. Phil sought solace in whisky, and started hanging around the Square looking more than usually rough. Finally, after one particularly heavy drinking session, he managed to corner Kathy for long enough to propose marriage to her – and, to his astonishment, she accepted.

Don't worry – Kathy won't be smiling for long

First of all there was the small business of his wife Nadia to deal with (she disappeared to Germany with £1000 of Phil's money in her pocket), and the way was clear for a Walford wedding. Sharon wasn't best pleased; she'd renounced Phil, but didn't want anyone else to have him, and went round to his flat one night hell-bent on getting him back into bed. They kissed, but Phil suddenly remembered he was engaged, and threw her out. Emboldened by this rare moment of nobility, Phil announced that he and Kathy were going to hold a real humdinger of an engagement party. Even they, however, couldn't have predicted just what a humdinger it was going to be.

Sharongate

The storyline that came to an explosive climax in late October 1994 started innocently enough. Sharon had put her dalliance with Phil behind her – or at least, that's what she was telling everyone – and was getting on with the job of being Mrs Grant Mitchell, landlady of the Queen Vic. She and Grant were even thinking of starting a family. But then Michelle's boyfriend, Geoff the Lecturer, had the bright idea of interviewing local girls for a book about 'the social and economic importance of women in the East End'. Sharon was up for it, on condition that Michelle conducted the interview – and so, one autumn evening while a drag queen called Dolly Davenport was performing downstairs in the bar, Sharon spilled her guts to Michelle's all-too-efficient tape recorder. She recalled her childhood, her problems with her parents, her chequered love life, her devotion to Grant… and, prompted by Michelle, her affair with Phil. And then, like you do, she forgot that she'd left the incriminating tape in the machine.

Grant found the tape, pocketed it and decided to give it a listen. The anticipation lasted for weeks, as Grant's car stereo broke and was finally fixed. Then, on the night of Phil and Kathy's engagement party, he nipped over to the Three Feathers to borrow a barrel of beer from his mate Dave, and finally got to listen to the tape. What he heard came as a bit of a shock.

Such a shock, in fact, that he burst into the Vic in mute fury, stopped the music and put the tape on, so that all the world could hear Sharon's drunken confession. That certainly got a reaction: Kathy slapped Sharon's face and called her a slut, while Grant stalked Phil and beat the living daylights out of him in the Arches. Phil was left in a pool of blood in the inspection pit.

He didn't die, of course, but there was a lot of anguish over his hospital bed. Grant somehow got off scot free, and returned to the Vic to make Sharon's life hell, branding her 'the pub whore' and humiliating her in ever more inventive ways. Eventually Sharon could stand it no longer. She signed the divorce papers on Christmas Day (eerily reminiscent of the Den and Angie divorce-papers scene in 1986) and left Albert Square in a taxi.

Ricky and Bianca

We knew the Jackson family were trouble from the moment they arrived on the Square, but nobody could have predicted what a one-woman disaster area Bianca was going to be. After nearly having an affair with her own father, David, she set her sights on Ricky, then in his prime as a Brandoesque grease monkey, and before long they were scouring the Square for places in which to consummate their passion. The parents disapproved, naturally, which only served to push the star-crossed lovers closer. Despite Ricky's regular, inexplicable absences from Walford, the couple defied their elders and by the end of the year were living openly together.

Ricky Butcher with Bianca Jackson (Patsy Palmer)

Dangerous when wet: Cindy with Matt the lifeguard

Ian and Cindy

Ian found his true vocation in 1994 as a total sleazeball, operating as a 'financial adviser' or, in plain English, a loan shark. He became so obsessed with his dirty business, and with hounding Tricky Dicky out of the Square, that he neglected Cindy, who was finding motherhood less enchanting than it's cracked up to be. This was a big mistake. Cindy quickly found distractions at the local leisure centre, where her eye was caught by Matt the lifeguard – an Adonis in shorts. After months of frustration, Matt and Cindy took the plunge at the end of the year. Ian, blissfully unaware that history was repeating itself so soon, decided that being a usurer wasn't really for him, and decided to open a chip shop instead.

Also...

▶ Gita discovers Sanjay in bed with her sister Meena, and throws him out... ▶ David Wicks turns up on his mother Pat's doorstep, on the run from the CSA and underage sex charges, and promptly starts pursuing Bianca, his own daughter... ▶ Natalie's phantom boyfriend Derek is exploded... ▶ Pauline's aunt Nellie comes to live chez Fowler, causing distress wherever she goes... ▶ Steve falls in love with hairdresser Della, but is distressed to discover that she is a lesbian, and has a girlfriend called Binnie... ▶ Nigel and Debbie get married... ▶ Pat and Michelle compete for Geoff... ▶ Mark meets Ruth at an Aids hospice, and they start a relationship... ▶ Robbie adopts a stray dog, Wellard...

Sanjay Kapoor (Deepak Verma)

A dog's life: Grant with Frieda, Robbie with Wellard

Arthur welcomes Auntie Nellie (Elizabeth Kelly) to Albert Square

EVERYONE TALKED ABOUT…

Sharongate

It remains one of *EastEnders*' finest moments, the perfect blend of high drama and low comedy. Sharon had confessed her adultery with her brother-in-law to Michelle, who had tape recorded the whole sordid monologue – like you do. Grant discovered the tape in the car stereo, and decided to liven up Phil and Kathy's engagement party by whacking it on the pub stereo and doing a spot of DJing. Within hours, Phil lay near death at the bottom of the Arches' inspection pit…

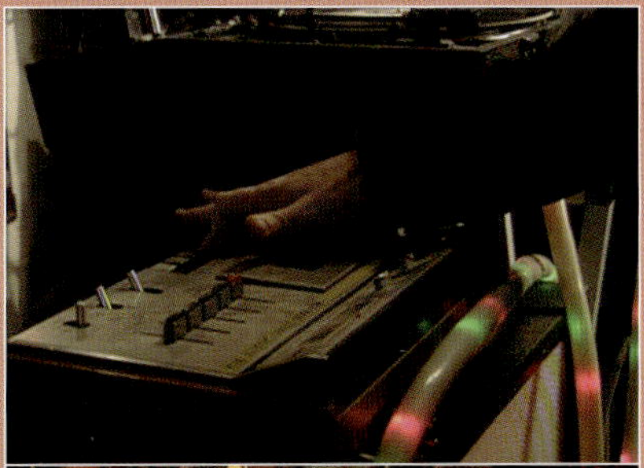

Any requests? Grant hits the decks with a recording that really gets the party started

Kathy learns that her fiancé has been up to no good with her future sister-in-law. Sharon develops a tense, nervous headache

The battle of the blondes: Kathy scores a decisive victory by smacking Sharon round the chops and callng her a slut. Result!

Grant deals with the situation in the only way he knows how, with a spot of mindless violence

Ricky, Bianca and Natalie

Surprisingly, Ricky Butcher found himself the object of a great deal of female attention in 1995. His clandestine relationship with Bianca was now common knowledge – but Bianca had a low boredom threshold, and was soon neglecting Ricky, leaving him vulnerable to predatory minxes like Natalie, her so-called best friend. Natalie lost no time in manoeuvring Ricky into bed – he always was easily led – and kept him under her thumb throughout the early part of the year. The strain of having to satisfy not one but two Walford women started to tell on Ricky, who took to hanging around the Arches pasty-faced and dark-eyed. It couldn't last; eventually Natalie engineered things so Bianca discovered her with Ricky in *flagrante delicto*, and the flame-haired woman scorned was instantly transformed into a cockney fury. She threw chips in Ricky's face and cut up all his clothes, slapped Natalie in public and eventually persuaded her to leave Walford for her own good (but not before loyal Robbie had sprayed the word 'slag' on her front door).

Natalie left Walford with her tail between her legs, unmasked as a dirty man-stealer and love rat. And despite the fact that Ricky left her on such a sour note, claiming she was only ever good for one thing, she would be back to get her man in years to come.

Romantic Roy (Tony Caunter) woos Pat in Paris

Pat, Roy and Frank

Abandoned by Frank, Pat reinvented herself as a mainstay of the car lot with son David, and looked forward to a life of industrious celibacy. It wasn't long, however, before yet another bee was buzzing around her honeypot, this time in the unlikely shape of Roy Evans. Early attempts to win Pat's favours with presents and holidays got him nothing but refusals; Pat later softened and went on the offered cruise after all, making it quite clear there would be no hanky-panky.

Hanky-panky was always going to be in short supply where Roy was concerned; when Pat finally decided that the time was right to surrender to his manly desires, she learned that Roy was impotent, and could offer nothing more than a passionate friendship. This was bad news for a woman of Pat's prodigious appetite – and yet, relieved to discover that for the first time in her life a man wanted her for something other than sex, she decided to give him the benefit of the doubt, and allowed him to move in with her in November. This was bad timing; no sooner had Roy placed his toothbrush by the sink than a letter had arrived from a psychiatric nurse in Bristol, announcing that Frank had suffered from a complete breakdown but was now ready to see his wife and family again.

Frank turned up at Pat's on Christmas Day ('Hello, babe…') but was swiftly given his marching orders. He wandered off into the night once more, but this time Ricky was on his tail.

Sharon

Sharon turned up out of the blue in March, landing unannounced on Michelle's doorstep with a suitcase in her hand. This was a very different Sharon from the whipped dog that had left the Square three months earlier; now she was confident and chic, courted by men in red Porsches, and even able to stand up to Peggy, who took over as reigning landlady of the Vic in July. When Peggy discovered the real reason for Sharon's abrupt departure the previous year, she delivered the first of many public slaps to pass between the two women in years to come; this one was administered in the market.

Sharon, however, was not so easily cowed, and her gutsy behaviour earned the grudging respect of Grant, who found himself coming over all soppy every time Sharon trotted into the bar on her high heels. It seemed for a moment as if Mr and Mrs Mitchell might once again be a going concern; Sharon even got Grant to admit as much, squeezing a declaration of love out of him by June. But it was all an act; beneath her cuddly exterior, Sharon was a woman bent on revenge, and she confessed to Michelle that she was going to make Grant sorry he had ever been born. To this end she lured him to a hotel, allowed him to have his wicked way and gave him to understand that a proposal of remarriage would not fall on deaf ears. Grant, full of the joys, was ready to pop the question at the Vic's big quiz night, and Sharon was ready to turn him down in front of his entire family. In the end, however, she couldn't go through with it, and beat a hasty retreat in a black cab, headed for America. That was the last we would see of Sharon for a very long time.

Michelle

Sharon wasn't the only original EastEnder to fly the coop in 1995; by the end of the year, her best friend Michelle had joined her in the USA. Michelle had led a miserable life ever since her marriage to Lofty – well, ever since the beginning of the show, really – and she began to realise in 1995 that there might be more to life than sleeping with married men in Walford. She made a half-hearted attempt to marry Geoff, her university lecturer, even going as far as to agree to go all the way up Scotland to start a new life with him. But after blowing hot and cold for several weeks, Michelle and Geoff realised that they would never be Mr and Mrs Barnes. It was left to Geoff to call the wedding off; Michelle, for all her many virtues, was always a coward when it came to these things.

After this, Michelle was a woman adrift. She flung herself at her married boss Gary, who very sensibly turned her down. Even her own brother turned against her, telling her that she was nothing more than a serial adulterer who would never form a lasting relationship. And so, when the opportunity arose for Michelle to take up a job in Birmingham, Alabama, she shook the dust of Walford from her shoes and left for good.

But she had one little job to do before she left, and that was to stand up to that big bully Grant. Michelle had never forgiven Grant for the way he treated Sharon, and Grant had never forgiven Michelle for driving a wedge between him and his wife. The stage was set for a *High Noon*-style confrontation late one night in the Vic, where the two antagonists met, quarrelled…and ended up having sex, like you do. When Michelle left

Michelle and Grant, moments before the conception of Mark Junior

Walford for her new life in America, she was carrying Grant's child.

Arthur and the Flowering Wilderness Fund

The *EastEnders* scriptwriters obviously got a perverse thrill out of making Arthur Fowler suffer. Not content with the Christmas Club scandal, or the Mrs Hewitt affair, they drove him in 1995 to his lowest-ever ebb after the disappearance of the Flowering Wilderness Fund.

It all started innocently enough: Arthur was elected secretary of the allotment committee, and started raising money to create a new eco-friendly urban garden. He hadn't counted, however, on the sinister manipulations of his old friend Willy Roper, whom he met at a funeral and who instantly started taking an interest in Arthur's financial dealings. By the end of the year, Arthur's tedious fundraising efforts had amassed £20,000 – enough to tempt Willy Roper to crime. Taking advantage of Arthur's brutish trust in human nature, he got him to sign the money off into various different accounts – and then left Arthur to face the music when the 20 grand was declared missing. Faced with a police investigation and persecution by the *Walford Gazette*, Arthur immediately started acting like a criminal, and to nobody's surprise he was arrested and sent to prison. This was too much for his already feeble mind, and he ended the year behind bars, a gibbering wreck, while Wicked Willy rubbed his hands in glee.

David and Cindy

The moment Cindy and David clapped eyes on each other, we knew there was going to be trouble. Not

Arthur does porridge

Dirty linen: Cindy and David (Michael French) wash theirs in public

only were they the two most attractive people in the show – they were also equally matched in cunning and deceit. It started innocently enough, with a little flirtation in the market; before long, however, Cindy was making regular trips to the Portacabin to confide in her new 'friend'. When Cindy saw David running around a football pitch in shorts, the die was cast. From that moment on, she turned to jelly every time she saw him, and provided a convenient outlet for David, whose hormones were already in a spin due to his incestuous lust for his own daughter, Bianca.

David played it cool for as long as he could, but by the autumn he had a full-blown case of *Fatal Attraction* on his hands. Cindy had taken to hanging round the car lot scratching her initials in the paintwork; it was only a matter of time before he was calling round at the chip shop for a good deal

EVERYONE TALKED ABOUT…

Gruesome twosome

Some cockney couplings should just never have happened, and this was one of them. Grant and Michelle had always hated each other, and took sides over that whole nasty Sharon business – so what did they do? They got drunk one night in the Vic and ended up having sex. The consequences of this (Michelle got pregnant) were so diabolical that she left Walford forever, and gave birth to a son, Mark, whom we would never see. And whom Grant, more to the point, would never meet.

'And another thing…' Michelle gives Grant a piece of her mind (again)

The old 'hand on the doorhandle' trick; Michelle wavers as Grant offers her a drink

Having sampled the entire stock of the Queen Vic, it's debatable whether Grant and Michelle really knew what they were doing

A glassy-eyed Grant makes his move. This was not the first time Michelle had conceived in the pub

Hard to believe that Cindy would leave Ian for another man

more than a portion of cod. Ian nearly caught the guilty lovers on more than one occasion, but thanks to David's quick-wittedness, and Ian's absorption in pub quizzes, he never quite twigged.

Eventually, it all proved too much for Cindy, who escaped to her mum's in Devon for a few weeks to calm down. When she returned to Walford in the autumn, nothing much had changed, apart from the fact that Ian had grown a revolting moustache. Cindy gave David an ultimatum: take me away from all this, or leave me alone. When he hesitated, she tried, briefly, to be a good wife to Ian and a mother to her children. It didn't last.

Also...

▶ Bianca's friend Tiffany turns up in Albert Square, and gets a job in the Vic... ▶ Wellard takes drugs at a party, and suffers from a hangover... ▶ David reveals to Bianca that he is her father... ▶ Della and Binnie go to live in Spain together... ▶ Ruth and Mark get married in Scotland, but soon start arguing about whether or not to have children... ▶ Phil and Kathy are reconciled after Sharongate and get married, and by the end of the year she is carrying his child... ▶ Grant learns the secret of Mark's HIV status... ▶ Big parties are held in Albert Square to celebrate the 50th anniversary of VE Day... ▶ Debbie is killed in a road accident, and Nigel fights for custody of Clare... ▶ Phil and Grant go to Torremolinos to rescue sister Sam from a life of vice... ▶ Ricky still has feelings for Sam... ▶ Kathy's older brother Ted Hills arrives in Walford with his two children, Tony and Sarah, on the run from a murder charge... ▶ A gas explosion wrecks the Jacksons' house... ▶ Robbie Williams appears in the background of the Queen Vic in September...

Nasty Bits of Work

They would sell their own grandmothers for the price of a pint – and, in fact, some of them have done just that. Meet Walford's least likeable villains.

Nick Cotton

He's in a league of his own, of course. Nick Cotton got the ball rolling by committing *EastEnders*' very first murder in 1985 (he killed Reg Cox), and since then he's done it all – usually to his own mother. He blackmailed Kathy over her first rape, he dealt drugs to minors, he put Mary on the game, he committed several burglaries and even sold dodgy salmon. His most spectacular crime was the attempted poisoning of Dot in 1990; he failed that time, but inadvertently killed his own son in 2001. What will he think of next?

Ian Beale

Ian 'Squeal' Beale, as he was known at school, is without doubt the most unpleasant character ever to stalk the streets of Walford. Lacking Nick Cotton's honest-to-goodness villainy, he's nevertheless made life hell for everyone who ever got close to him. He turned his back on his own mother when she was raped. He's lied, cheated and blackmailed to get money. Inexplicably, women keep marrying him, but he's alienated them all, Cindy, Mel and even dozy Laura. Thankfully, we've often seen his come-uppance; nobody has been beaten up or let down as often as Ian – or deserved it as much.

Frank Butcher

For all his twinkly-eyed cockney charm, Frank was never more than a second-rate conman and love-rat. He rolled into town to pick up the pieces with his teenage sweetheart Pat, and managed to break her cast-iron heart. He ruined his children's lives by being not only absent but also totally dishonest. And for what he did to poor Peggy – winning her, dumping her and then conning her out of a great deal of money after faking his own death – he deserves our utter contempt.

James Willmott-Brown

Nobody likes a toff in Walford, so it was inevitable that the posh-talking public schoolboy would turn out to be a psychotic beast. He smooth-talked Kathy into a compromising position, and when she said 'no', he raped her. Despite his protestations of innocence, it turned out that he had form for the same offence – and when he came crawling back, asking her to 'start again', he was given short shrift.

Trevor Morgan

A monster from north of the border, the smooth-talking wife-beating Scot made Little Mo's life hell until she took matters (and an iron) into her own hands. Even then, Trevor wouldn't lie down, and returned to terrorise the Slater family. The memory of his chilling stare haunts the Square long after he was burned to death.

Also:

- ▷ Terry Raymond, bigamist and child-beater
- ▷ Willy Roper, framed Arthur then tried to seduce his wife
- ▷ Harry Slater, paedophile
- ▷ Mehmet Osman, drug dealer and pimp
- ▷ Charlie Cotton, bigamist and thief
- ▷ Alistair Matthews, bogus priest and sexual hypocrite
- ▷ George Palmer, gangsta
- ▷ Graham from the Vic, Little Mo's rapist

1996

Wife, mother and would-be murderess – Cindy with her hapless children

Cindy and David

This was the year in which Cindy Beale nearly did the world a big favour by disposing once and for all of her whingeing husband Ian. The storyline that climaxed in October had been simmering for months and the heat was turned up a notch in January when David and Cindy sorted out their problems and resumed their regular trysts in the Deals on Wheels Portacabin. That was their love-nest of choice, but for a bit of variety they arranged regular sessions in Barry's flat, and occasionally popped out for a spot of al fresco by the canal. On one occasion Cindy dragged David off to Essex, on the pretext of looking for a new family home for her, Ian and the kids, and had sex with him while the estate agent's back was turned. She always was a class act.

It couldn't last, of course. Cindy was applying pressure to David to leave Walford with her – but, despite his promises, David just couldn't face up to his responsibilities. He bought time by encouraging Ian to try marriage guidance, and kept his options open by resuming his ancient affair with Carol – as if her life wasn't complicated enough already. Eventually, even Ian twigged that something suspicious was going on; there's only so many times you can catch your wife alone with another man before you start to worry. And so, in typically weaselly style, Ian hired a private detective to follow Cindy around. The proof – a live broadcast of Cindy and David all over each other – was a little too graphic even for Ian, who flipped and started shouting impotent threats to anyone in the Square who would listen.

Ian wasn't the only one who had engaged professional help, however. Cindy had overheard David and Barry discussing how cheap and easy it was to hire a hitman, and so, with alarming ease, she got hold of an unsavoury character called John Valecue, who agreed to rub out her husband for the bargain price of £1500. Cindy borrowed the money from David (allegedly for a flat) and then spent weeks dithering over whether she wanted Ian dead or just badly hurt. When Ian threatened to deprive her of contact with the children and forced her to return to the marital home, Cindy decided that death was probably the more attractive option.

Cindy was a cat on a hot tin roof that day in October when the hit was scheduled to happen. Just when she'd decided that, after all, she'd rather not be a murderer, a car pulled up alongside her and Ian and a shot rang out. Ian crumpled to the floor – but he was only winged, and recovered. Under pressure from the police (and, presumably, racked with disappointment about Ian's survival), Cindy decided to flee. David helped her to get her two sons to Waterloo International (she couldn't snatch Lucy in time), but declined to board the Eurostar with her. Cindy ended 1996 living a shadowy life in Paris; Walford was a far duller place without her.

The Death of Arthur

Arthur emerged from prison in May a broken man. He had been cleared of misappropriating the Flowering Wilderness funds – that, as we knew all along, had been done by Willy Roper, who emerged as a bug-eyed lunatic intent on seducing the luscious Pauline on a trip to Jersey. What should have been a triumphant return to Walford for Arthur soon turned to tragedy, however. It seems he had recently received a nasty blow to the head during a disturbance in prison and, only a few days after his release, collapsed on the allotments and finally died in hospital. The funeral was delayed pending an inquest, but the jury eventually returned a verdict of accidental death, much to the disgust of Mark and Pauline, who felt that the prison services neglected to seek proper medical help for Arthur at the time.

As one Fowler departed this life, another arrived: Michelle, still safely tucked away in the USA, gave birth to a son, Mark Junior. Pauline urged her to come home and raise the baby in Walford, and even went all the way to America to press her case. Michelle very sensibly declined – she was staying put with her new baby and a new husband. Grant would never know that he was the father.

Mark's HIV Status

Mark had thus far managed to keep his HIV status a secret known only by his immediate circle. In 1996, however, the Walford grapevine did its work, and soon it was common knowledge. It all came out when Kathy and Phil's baby Ben fell ill with meningitis; in a panic, his parents jumped to the conclusion that Mark was to blame, and soon his condition was being broadcast to the entire Square.

Mark on his stall

The depth of ignorance surrounding HIV and Aids in Walford must have come as a shock to the health profession. Peggy led the armies of ignorance, boycotting Mark's fruit and veg stall and ostentatiously throwing away some lemons she'd bought from him. Pauline sprang to her son's defence, and indulged in a slapfight with Peggy in the Vic – but even she couldn't defuse public prejudice, and Mark returned home one day to find the words 'AIDS SCUM' daubed across his wall.

This was too much for him, and he decided to present the world with a few facts. Mark's big scene happened, like all the best things in *EastEnders*, in the bar of the Queen Vic, where he set the locals right about HIV and confronted his delightful neighbours with their own bigotry. Peggy remained uncertain, but was forced to realise that Mark might appreciate a bit of support when, at the end of the year, she was diagnosed with breast cancer.

Joe (Paul Nicholls) looks into the abyss

Joe Wicks

A grubby, but nonetheless extremely attractive, young man turned up in Albert Square in March, asking a lot of questions in a thick northern accent about David Wicks. This turned out, of course, to be David's long-lost son Joe, on whom the feckless father had walked out eight years ago, leaving his mother Lorraine to bring him and his sister Karen up alone. Lorraine was hot on Joe's heels – and she had an unwelcome piece of news for David. Their daughter Karen had been killed in a car accident for which Joe blamed himself (quite unnecessarily). She took Joe back to Bolton, much to David's relief; he had his hands full with Cindy at the time.

Joe, however, was not so easily put off, and returned to Walford in May, determined to rebuild a relationship with his father. But it soon turned out that Joe was a severely troubled teenager. His guilt about Karen's death turned into a full-blown mental breakdown, which escalated throughout the summer. He became obsessed with the concept of 'evil', even, at one point, carving the word into his chest. He started playing with fire, leaving dead cats under his bed and dousing himself in lighter fuel on Bonfire Night. None of this was helped by drippy Sarah Hills, who rejected Joe's advances (was she insane herself?) and tried, instead, to get him to go to church with her. Religion was one thing this young man did not need, and by the end of the year he was clinically barking. He more or less kidnapped David, trapping him in their flat and boarding up the windows in an attempt to make him stay with him. David's response was very much in character: instead of remaining to support his troubled son, he disappeared into the night. Finally, after a few more desperate moments, Joe was taken to hospital to receive treatment.

Tiffany (Martine McCutcheon) and Grant

Tiffany and Grant

Tiffany, like all the initially gutsy, independent women of Walford, revealed that she had a broad masochistic streak when she fell for the world's most unsuitable man, Grant Mitchell. They bonded over drinks and confidences in June, and spent the night together – but agreed, rightly, that they would not be good for each other. Tiffany flitted on to the next man, Tony, dragging him off to a hotel just a few nights later in an attempt to straighten him out sexually. This led to a nice little affair which foundered spectacularly over the summer when Tiffany found Tony in bed with her brother, Simon.

Stung by this discovery, she rushed straight into the arms of Grant and told him that she was

EVERYONE TALKED ABOUT…

The hitman...and her

Okay, Cindy Beale was an adulterous homewrecker and an unfit mother, but nobody can really blame her for attempting to murder Ian. In her defence, she did have moments of bad conscience in the weeks leading up to the hit, and actually changed her mind at the last moment, but by then it was too late. This was the beginning of a very long end for Cindy, who fled to France, taking two of the kids with her, and later died in prison, depriving *EastEnders* of one of its greatest villains.

Cindy faces another day of being Mrs Ian Beale with fortitude

The realisation that she may soon be a widow dawns on her, and her spirits lift

A shot rings out, and Cindy attempts to look a) surprised and b) upset. She succeeds in neither

Missed! Ian, still very much alive, hits the deck

pregnant (although she omitted to mention that he might very well not be the father). Grant, who had always wanted a child of his own (and didn't know that he'd just had one, by Michelle!) was overjoyed, and whisked Tiffany away to Paris for a quickie wedding. Married life soon soured, however; Tiffany was not the first to discover that the job of being Mrs Grant Mitchell was not a pleasant one. By December they were rowing constantly, and by Christmas he'd grown violent. Tiffany became terrified of his reaction if he discovered that the baby might not be his.

When Grant found out that there was some doubt about the paternity, he flipped his lid, threw Tiffany out and called her every name under the sun. The fact that he was already committing adultery with Lorraine seemed to make no difference.

Tony and Simon

Tony Hills started his Walford life as a dodgy drug-dealer with a penchant for Tiffany. Little did his neighbours know, however, that he was sneaking off to gay bars at every opportunity, flirting with men and then bolting when they tried to go to bed with him. And so, when Tiffany's openly gay brother Simon turned up in Walford, on the run from a violent, abusive boyfriend, Tony became understandably nervous.

Love came slowly for Simon and Tony. When Tony was beaten up by drug dealers, it was Simon who tended to his wounds – but he froze when he learned that his Good Samaritan was gay, and nearly jumped out of his skin when he saw Simon coming out of the bathroom in a pair of boxer shorts. Things came to a head in August, when a group of young Walfordians went on a sanity break to Blackpool. Simon found Tony hanging around in gay bars, and, after a long heart-to-heart, they kissed. Tony was delighted at the time, but Tiffany ruined the moment by arriving to tell them she was keeping her baby. On his return home Tony got cold feet and started blaming Simon for leading him astray. After a brief separation, they became lovers in September and confronted a disbelieving Walford with their relationship. Tony was happy – for a while, at least. By the end of the year, he was beginning to wonder if he was, after all, bisexual.

Also...

▶ The car lot is burned down for a second time; this time Barry is the culprit, attempting to scare off Frank but nearly killing Phil in the process… ▶ Pat and Roy marry… ▶ Sam tries to get Ricky back, but finally admits defeat and leaves Walford for good… ▶ Sarah overcomes kleptomania and gets religion instead… ▶ Kathy gives birth to a son, Ben, who gets meningitis and is left with impaired hearing… ▶ Phil's drinking develops into full-blown alcoholism… ▶ Alan and Carol get married, but he immediately starts an affair with Frankie, a singer… ▶ Carol finds comfort in the arms of David… ▶ A riot in the Square over plans to destroy the playground results in the arrest of 'the Walford Six'… ▶ Peggy starts going out with dodgy George Palmer, and is diagnosed with breast cancer in December...

Neil Clark (Alistair Matthews) with Sarah Hills (Daniela Denby-Ashe)

Extra-marital Affairs

There's only one good reason to get married in Albert Square - and that's so you can immediately start having an affair. Here are some highlights of East End adultery.

Den and Jan, 1985

He was the sexy wide-boy, she was the glacial posh mistress, and together they made poor Angie's life hell for years. Finally Jan had had enough, and married her Italian boyfriend.

Den and Michelle, 1985

He was the sexy wide-boy, she was his adoptive daughter's best friend, and together they made a baby.

Angie and Tony, Andy, etc., 1985/6

Angie got her revenge on Den by flirting with every man in Walford, and actually had full-blown affairs with several of them. They did not make her happy.

Charlie Cotton, Rose and Joan Leggett, 1988

Not content with being bigamously married to both Dot and Joan Leggett, Charlie was also living with Dot's half-sister Rose.

Michelle and Danny, 1989

Michelle had a fatal taste for married men: Den, then Danny, who also had an inconvenient wife he wasn't going to leave.

Cindy and Wicksy, 1989/90

The first of Cindy's great betrayals of Ian - even before they were married, she resumed her on/off relationship with Simon. The result was a son, Steven.

Sharon and Phil, 1992

Adultery raised to the level of high drama here: Sharon's fatal attraction for the other Mitchell brother brought her house of cards tumbling down.

Arthur and Mrs Hewitt, 1992

Dubbed the 'Bonk of the Year' by the tabloids, Arthur's stolen afternoons of passion with lonely, drunken Christine were truly touching.

Sanjay and Meena, 1994
Another of the great in-law affairs dealt a fatal blow to Sanjay and Gita's marriage.

Cindy and Matt, 1994
Matt the horny lifeguard was a temptation that Cindy could not resist.

Natalie and Ricky, 1995
Natalie couldn't stand to see her so-called friend, Bianca, happily married... And she got him back in 2003.

Grant and Michelle, 1995
After screaming about how much they hated each other, Grant and Michelle ended the evening with a quick bit of sex.

David and Cindy, 1995
Another of the great adulteries – and another for which you couldn't blame Cindy, being married to the awful Ian.

Alan and Frankie, 1996
After a long relationship and a quickie marriage to Carol, Alan decided he'd better have an affair too. Enter Frankie, the predatory pub singer.

Tony and Polly, 1997
Okay, Tony and Simon weren't technically married; but Tony's affair with Polly shows that you don't have to be straight to be unfaithful. Simon retaliated with Chris.

Phil and Lorna, 1997
Phil was still married to Kathy when he started a dangerous liaison with mentally unstable fellow alcoholic Lorna.

Kathy and Alex, 1998
Likewise, Kathy was still married to Phil when she began to realise that she might like to be a vicar's wife.

Louise and Grant, 1998
Of all Grant's ridiculous affairs, this quickie with his own wife's mother was probably the most distasteful.

Irene and Troy, 1999
After trying yoga and chanting, Irene discovered that what really put a spring back in her step was regular, vigorous sex with a man half her age.

Bianca and Dan Sullivan, 1999
Bianca was still married to Ricky when she rekindled a teenage romance with big man Dan. Only trouble was, he was her mother's boyfriend.

Pat and Frank, 2000

These lovebirds never could keep their hands off each other, even when on holiday in Spain with their respective spouses, Roy and Peggy.

Sharon and Ross, 2001

Sharon was very smug when her new boyfriend followed her back to Walford in 2001; only trouble was, he had a wife and it wasn't her.

Ian and Janine, 2002

Ian's marriage to Laura was never exactly a bed of roses, but going for a night of paid-for passion with Janine was a low point.

Lynne and Jason, 2002

When she wasn't out canoodling with Beppe, Lynne liked to cheat on her husband Garry with her old flame Jason.

Den and Kate, 2004

Den seduced yet another lady in the Square, not long after his secret wife, Chrissie, had agreed to take him back. His mistress? Chrissie's new business partner, Kate.

Marriages

Nobody takes the state of matrimony very seriously in Walford. Here's a list of the main weddings over 20 years – and what happened to them!

▷ Michelle and Lofty, 1986 (they split) ▷ Frank and Pat, 1989 (he ran off without a trace) ▷ Ian and Cindy, 1989 (she tried to murder him) ▷ Sharon and Grant, 1991 (she left after sleeping with his brother) ▷ Ricky and Sam, 1991 (they eloped, but she left him) ▷ Mark and Gill, 1992 (she died soon after) ▷ Phil and Nadia, 1993 (for the passport) ▷ Nigel and Debbie, 1994 (she died in a car crash) ▷ Ruth and Mark, 1995 (they split) ▷ Phil and Kathy, 1995 (his drinking and affairs drove her away) ▷ Roy and Pat, 1996 (after several splits, he died) ▷ Alan and Carol, 1996 (he had an affair) ▷ Grant and Tiff, 1996 (she got run over) ▷ Ricky and Bianca, 1997 (she had an affair with her mother's boyfriend) ▷ Irene and Terry, 1999 (she left him in Spain) ▷ Peggy and Frank, 1999 (he had an affair with Pat, then left) ▷ Ian and Mel, 1999 (she left him on their wedding night) ▷ Barry and Natalie, 1999 (she left him for Ricky) ▷ Steve and Mel, 2001 (he died) ▷ Laura and Ian, 2001 (she apparently got pregnant by Garry) ▷ Lynne and Garry, 2001 (both had affairs) ▷ Dot and Jim, 2002 (still together!) ▷ Mark and Lisa, 2002 (she fled to Portugal) ▷ Little Mo and Billy, 2002 (still married, on paper) ▷ Barry and Janine, 2003 (he fell off a cliff) ▷ Alfie and Kat, 2003 (no longer together)

Love for Sale

Practically everyone in Walford appears to have slept with everyone else at one time or another. Here's a few that have made a career of it.

▷ Punk Mary was a part-time stripper and was lured on to the game by Mehmet Osman and Nick Cotton ▷ Donna Ludlow resorted to prostitution in order to pay for her drug habit ▷ Disa O'Brien followed a well-beaten path from artist's model to prostitute; luckily, Diane Butcher just stuck to modelling ▷ Pat was often to be found on the fringes of the oldest profession ▷ Sam Mitchell toyed with the idea of nude modelling and did a spot of pole-dancing in dodgy Spanish clubs ▷ Mandy Salter followed in her mother's footsteps by trying a bit of casual whoring up in King's Cross ▷ Nina Harris was horrified when one of her former clients turned up in the Square to remind her of a time when she wasn't just a barmaid ▷ Zoe Slater was hopeless as a prostitute; she threw up on her first client, and ran out on her second, leaving Madame Roxy in a fuming temper. Kelly, however, was less squeamish ▷ Janine Butcher discovered a handy way to pay for her cocaine addiction by sleeping with her dealer, then his friends, then with anyone who'd have her ▷ Mo Harris is the Square's most unlikely sex worker, but she made a tidy sum out of her 'Miss Whiplash' S&M chatline in 2002

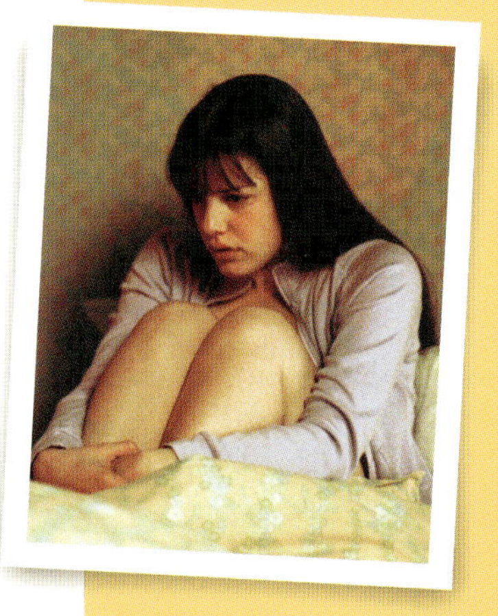

Walford: Gay Pride?

Considering the number of people who have lived in and around Albert Square, there've been precious few lesbian and gay characters in *EastEnders*. Here's some that were – or nearly were...

▷ Colin Russell dated barrow-boy Barry (who then decided he was straight) and then Guido ▷ Sam Mitchell had a gay best friend Jamie in 1990; he disappeared without a trace ▷ Michelle was so pally with landlady Rachel that the Square was abuzz with rumours that she was more than just a lodger ▷ Joe Wallace met Mark at the Terrence Higgins Trust in 1990, and did a brief stint in the Square. He died of Aids a few years later ▷ Della and Binnie were that rarest of all Walford visitors, an openly lesbian couple ▷ Simon knew he was gay from the word go; Tony couldn't make his mind up, but eventually decided that, on the whole, he was – maybe ▷ Fred Fonseca came out to a few raised eye brows as the Square's one and only gay GP ▷ Martin Fowler's sexuality has come under question a couple of times: first when he nearly snogged gay friend Craig, and second when he took a few too many driving lessons with Derek ▷ Derek the panto king surprised nobody when he told Pauline he was gay – but he had a wife and kids hidden away in his past ▷ Kelly revealed that she was interested in being much more than friends with Zoe on a rainsoaked Scottish heath

Lost Girls

Over the years, Albert Square has been littered with women who couldn't take the rough and tumble of life in the East End. Here are a few of our favourite broken blossoms.

Mary Smith

With her punk warpaint and ever-changing hairstyle, Mary may have looked as hard as nails – but actually she was a fragile little thing who wanted nothing more than to provide a good home for baby Annie. The fact is, she was a hopeless mother. She left Annie home alone (once in dangerous proximity to the fire) while she sold her body on the streets and dabbled in drugs. Rod the Roadie and Andy O'Brien seemed to offer some stability, but Mary could never get herself straightened out, and left Walford to inflict herself on other London boroughs.

Diane Butcher

You can't really blame Diane for running away from home, what with a father like Frank, but, boy, did she make a meal of it. She ended up living on the streets, almost getting lured into prostitution, and certainly doing a great deal more than modelling for her artist boyfriend. Later she turned up living in Bohemian squalor in Paris with a jazz musician and a baby (not his). We can only imagine what a mess she's made of her life since then.

Donna Ludlow

Tragic Donna didn't have the best start in life as the child of rape, instantly given up for adoption by her traumatised mother Kathy. But when she turned up in Walford, it was clear to all that she was a loon. She quickly established herself as a compulsive liar, and took to drugs and prostitution as if to the manner born. Finally she OD'd on Dot's couch, and was almost universally unmourned.

Disa O'Brien

Disa was to Diane as Kelly is to Zoe – the girl who really did go on the game. Diane rescued Disa from life on the streets, and even took her in when she gave birth in a cardboard box – but Disa didn't stick around to thank her. As soon as she'd got her abusive stepfather banged up, she was off.

Mandy Salter

The utterly poisonous Mandy was the daughter of a dodgy old lush that Pat had picked up in a hostess bar, and she arrived in Walford to work out some obscure grudge she held against the entire world. She lied, cheated and stole, she seduced gormless Ricky and Aidan, but when she tried to go on the game she just got beaten up by rival prostitutes.

Also:

- ▷ Nina, Irene's niece, trying to live down her prostitute past
- ▷ Kelly, another reformed bad girl with an uncertain future
- ▷ Vicki, conceived on the pub carpet, which proved to be a high point in her life
- ▷ Demi Miller, already a mother at 13

1997

A freshly christened Courtney shortly before her uncle Simon (Andrew Lynford) went mad, her mother died and her father disappeared

Grant and Tiffany

The birth of baby Courtney should have been a cause for celebration but, this being *EastEnders*, the little bundle of joy brought only misery to everyone concerned. Grant's male pride was wounded when he discovered that he might not be the child's father – and, long before the birth, he was telling Tiffany that he didn't love her and that he wanted a divorce (which he couldn't have before their first anniversary in November). Mere days before the birth in March, he was carrying on with Lorraine – but still managed to maintain his self-righteous stance.

Courtney was born by Caesarean section, and for a moment Grant appeared to soften towards his wife. But it didn't last; he ran back to Lorraine, beating his chest, refusing to accept that the child was his. A DNA test put the paternity question beyond all doubt: Grant was Courtney's father, God help her.

It would be nice to report that Grant knuckled down under this new responsibility, but the nearest he got to becoming a New Man was changing a single nappy. He found it impossible to break off with Lorraine, but contented himself with treating her just as badly as he was treating Tiffany. The latter had lost her dignity completely by the summer, begging him to love her and the baby; Grant responded by threatening to sue for custody of the child, and push her out of the picture altogether.

Somehow the warring Mitchells patched up their differences and decided to have a blessing ceremony in August, to make up for their quickie wedding the previous year. Their holiday in Paris did them good; while everyone else was splitting up, Grant and Tiffany seemed to draw closer (although he did offer sexual favours to Kathy, just to keep his hand in). This, however, was only a brief respite. By Christmas Grant had stepped back into character, and started terrorising Tiffany in her own home, breaking down doors, throwing her to the floor and cutting her head, all of which was witnessed by Courtney. Tiffany fled for refuge at Bianca's, but when Grant did those big puppy-dog eyes she came crawling back for more.

Phil and Kathy

Peggy Mitchell wondered, and not without reason, what she'd done to raise such a pair of rotten apples as Phil and Grant. While her younger son was beating seven bells out of his wife, her firstborn responded to the joys of new parenthood by hitting the bottle. Unable to cope with having to share Kathy with baby Ben, Phil gave in to his incipient drink problem and blossomed as a fully-fledged alcoholic. He was sent into terminal decline when the Arches was shut down by Trading Standards Officers. His love life collapsed, he fell in with a bad lot and got mugged for his troubles, and spent the rest of the year clutching his head in a permanent hangover.

As the year wore on, Phil's behaviour became increasingly erratic. He'd disappear on 48-hour benders, often turning up in police custody or with some dodgy woman on his arm. He snatched Ben and then left him near a fire. This was the last straw, and Phil made an honest attempt to kick the bottle and rebuild his marriage. Kathy took him back for a while, but it didn't last. When he returned to counselling in the summer, he promptly began an affair with a fellow alcoholic, Lorna, who started stalking him and soon made herself known to Kathy.

With their relationship in a tailspin, Phil and Kathy joined Grant and Tiffany on their Paris holiday in August. Their return to the city where their relationship had first been kindled all those years ago was not a success. He blurted out the truth about Lorna – and she responded by pulling off her wedding ring and chucking it into the Seine. That was too much for Phil, who disappeared, only to turn up in Albert Square sleeping rough, blaming Kathy for his decline and suggesting, with true Mitchell charm, that she was somehow responsible for being raped by Willmott-Brown. Kathy contemplated suicide, but sensibly hardened her heart against her abusive alcoholic husband and settled instead for the more wholesome charms of Alex the vicar, with whom she shared a Christmas kiss. Phil ended the year alone – as he so richly deserved.

Ricky and Bianca

Ricky and Bianca's relationship was always volatile, so it was nothing short of a miracle that the two of them tied the knot in April, with Frank watching disconsolately from the back of the church. Marriage seemed to settle them, and they spent the rest of the year in a state of comparative calm. But when Bianca discovered she was pregnant, she panicked, believing that Ricky did not want a family. She delayed telling him for as long as possible – and was delighted when the truth finally emerged that he was as keen to be a parent as she was.

Their joy was shortlived. A scan in November revealed that the baby had spina bifida and hydrocephalus, both incurable, both involving a great deal of pain. After a heartbreaking period of soul-searching, they decided to terminate the pregnancy, strengthened only by the hope that one day they would have a healthy baby.

Mr and Mrs Richard Butcher – but not for long

Sarah's 'Rape'

Sarah Hills sealed her reputation as one of Walford's least likeable characters by dropping practically the entire cast into one of the most unpleasant storylines ever to hit *EastEnders*. After dithering for months about her chaste relationship with Joe, she confided in her religious guru Alistair – who, of course, turned out to be a bad lot who was sleeping with one of his flock. Sarah, disillusioned by the church, got drunk and allowed Robbie (who had long adored her) to have sex with her – and then, when she realised what she had done, went completely nuts. She ran to Alistair in a state of distress, failed to get his forgiveness and then disappeared, explaining herself to no one.

In her absence, everyone got hold of the wrong end of the stick. Sarah's hateful father Ted convinced himself that his daughter had been raped – and if there was one subject upon which he was sore, it was the subject of his daughter's sexual purity. And so he went on the warpath, attacking any young man who had so much as shared a coffee with Sarah. At first his suspicions fell on Ricky, then Joe – and then, when he found out that Robbie was the man, he broke into his house and flung him down the stairs. Robbie was rushed into hospital and had to undergo a splenectomy, while Ted returned home, a proud father.

Sarah underwent a dark night of the soul on the streets of London in a bid to become the second Diane Butcher. She was saved by a sympathetic vicar, Alex, and came home to tell the truth about her night with Robbie. She then decided that she had better shop her father to the police for good measure; Ted was lucky to get off with a suspended sentence.

It looked at one point as if Ted was going to do Walford an immense favour by taking Sarah with him when he moved to Dubai, but unfortunately she hung around for a while longer, tormenting Joe with her emotional mitherings and even bringing her dodgy mother, Irene, on to the scene.

Terry and Irene

Irene Hills started out as the mother from hell. Flighty, bitchy and self-centred, she was a breath of fresh air when compared to her ghastly children, Tony and Sarah. She moved in with Tony and Simon and immediately came between them, cracking homophobic jokes and eventually splitting them up by revealing Tony's fling with colleague Polly. Payback was on the way, however – and when she met Simon and Tiffany's father, Terry, she met her match in dreadfulness. After sharing one too many boozy afternoons together, they began an affair just before Christmas. They tried, like a geriatric Romeo and Juliet, to keep it all a big secret – but nothing stays secret for long in Albert Square.

They deserve each other: Terry (Gavin Richards) and Irene (Roberta Taylor)

Ireland

One of *EastEnders*' flimsiest-ever storylines sent Pauline, Mark, Ruth and Ian off to Ireland, in search of Pauline's long-lost sister Maggie. We thought at first that she was only a half-sister, the result of an unlikely indiscretion by Lou. But, in fact, she was nothing more sinister than the result of premarital sex between Lou and her husband-to-be. Pauline was overjoyed to find a sister she'd never met; the rest of us were dismayed to meet Maggie and her dreadful brood, a bunch of Irish stereotypes complete with alcoholic father and roguish curly-haired charmer. Worst of all, said charmer, Conor, moved to Albert Square before the end of the year, along with his daughter Mary. She fell in love with

EVERYONE TALKED ABOUT...

The birth of Courtney

Grant Mitchell never found it easy to express affection, or indeed anything other than contempt, for the women in his life, but there was a brief moment in 1997 when he seemed almost to like his wife. And that was when she'd produced a child – the lovely Courtney. Don't be fooled, however: he was still having an affair with another woman, and would soon force the exhausted young mother to submit the child to a DNA test, so convinced was he that he was not the real father.

Tiffany recovers from a Caesarean section while the proud father sneaks to her bedside

Grant goes all gooey, and the viewing nation wonders if he's such a bad bloke after all

'You're right, Grant: she looks exactly like you!'

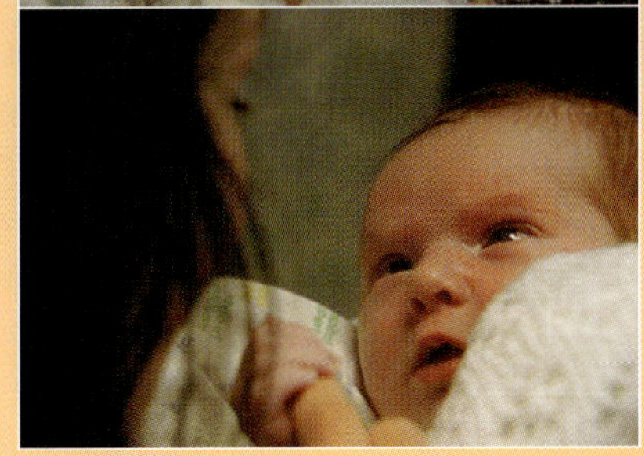

The not-very-newborn Courtney considers putting herself up for adoption

Mark with foster daughter Jessie

Joe Wicks, and even managed to manoeuvre him into bed – a situation to which Joe responded by leaving London for good.

Also...

▶ Tony has an affair with Frankie and Polly, but still gets gaybashed… ▶ Tony and Polly investigate the dodgy dealings of George and Annie Palmer… ▶ The Arthur Fowler Memorial Bench is raised in Albert Square… ▶ Billy Jackson witnesses an armed raid on a building society, and is kidnapped in order to prevent him from testifying… ▶ Carol Jackson is forced to leave the Square in order to protect Billy… ▶ Martin gets in trouble with an underage gang… ▶ Joe is diagnosed with schizophrenia and sectioned for 28 days… ▶ Sanjay and Gita try IVF treatment, while Mark and Ruth start fostering… ▶ Dot returns briefly, only to be held hostage by Nick's escaped cellmate Damion… ▶ Barry is stung by a con woman, Vanessa, for £140,000… ▶ Speedway-mania hits the young men of Walford… ▶ Ian tracks Cindy down in Italy, while Phil and Grant snatch back her two sons… ▶ Frank returns and is attracted to Peggy...

Con woman Vanessa Carlton (Adele Salem) with victim Barry

Death

Walford is a very dangerous place to live. If you're not run down by a car, you run the risk of being murdered by Nick Cotton, burned in one of the frequent fires, or succumbing to heart disease. And if all else fails, you could always contemplate suicide. Welcome to 20 years of East-End morbidity...

Reg Cox, 1985

EastEnders started on 19 February 1985 the way it meant to go on – with the discovery of a murder. There was an instant mystery about who had killed poor old loner Reg Cox, found at death's door in his flat when the door was kicked in. It later turned out – as was so often the case – that Nick Cotton was the culprit.

Hassan Osman, 1985

Probably the most traumatic of all *EastEnders* deaths was the demise of little Hassan, a victim of cot death. Sue and Ali's marriage never recovered from the grief and recrimination.

Andy O'Brien, 1986

Debs's boyfriend Andy was one of Albert Square's truly nice characters, so it was inevitable that he would meet a sticky end. After putting up with Debs's flirting with copper Roy Quick, and teaching Mary to read, and even having a fling with Angie, he was knocked down by a lorry and killed. But his goodness extended after death – he'd donated his kidneys.

Tom Clements, 1988

The poor old pot-man at the Vic had always held a torch for Dot – and, when he dropped dead in the pub toilets, they found a picture of the two of them in his wallet...

Benny Bloom, 1989

Ethel found romance late in life with the charming Benny Bloom, only to discover, when ringing him up for a date, that he'd passed away. He did, however, leave her £2000 in his will.

Donna Ludlow, 1989

One of the steepest declines in *EastEnders*' history was that of Kathy's daughter Donna, who arrived in the Square in 1988 as a slightly flaky young woman, but within the year had descended into prostitution and drug addiction. She died on Dot's sofa of a heroin overdose; she remains *EastEnders*' only successful suicide.

Eddie Royle, 1991

EastEnders' second murder mystery surrounded the hapless Eddie Royle, discovered with stab wounds in the Square early one morning in 1991. For a while, almost everyone was in the frame, most notably Clyde, who had found the body, and Grant. But in the end the perpetrator turned out to be – who else? – Nick Cotton.

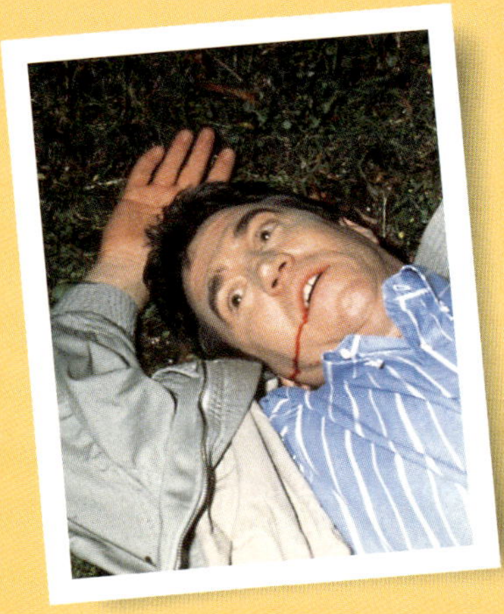

Stephanie Watson, 1992

Pat had had a couple of G&Ts on Christmas Eve, and was in a hurry to get home – but she was only doing 35mph when a teenage girl stepped in front of the car and got hit. The girl, Stephanie, died on New Year's Eve; Pat did time for manslaughter, and slumped into a depression from which it would take her many years to emerge.

Pete Beale, 1993

Pete was way out of his depth with Rose Chapman, the wife of a notorious gangster. His family didn't want anyone sniffing around 'their' Rose, and made that quite clear with a variety of death threats. Pete and Rose left London to start a new life – but that was cut short by an all-too-convenient car crash.

Joe Wallace, 1994

Mark got to know Joe through the Terrence Higgins Trust when he was first diagnosed with HIV. Joe wrote to him later, in 1994, to say he was dying in a hospice. Joe's early death terrified Mark, but there was some consolation: it was through Joe that he met Ruth, his wife-to-be.

Debbie Bates, 1995

Things were going far too well for Nigel in 1995; he'd finally got the girl, and was looking forward to some marital bliss. This was cut short when Debbie was killed in a road accident, leaving Nigel to fight for custody of her daughter, Claire.

Arthur Fowler, 1996

After a life of almost unrelieved grimness, Arthur fittingly collapsed on the allotments, with a confused look on his face. His sudden death may or may not have been the result of head injuries sustained during his recent spell in prison.

Tiffany Mitchell, 1998

Yet another pedestrian under yet another car – this time it was Tiffany, trying to get away from Grant, who collided with one of Frank's many motors. She died as she lived – gorgeously groomed, not a hair out of place.

Cindy Beale, 1998

After attempting to kill Ian Beale, Cindy deserved better than an ignominious death in a prison cell. She died giving birth to a daughter, from a bloodclot on her lung, and was buried in Devon – where her daughter, named after her mother, presumably still lives.

Saskia Duncan, 1999

Poor Saskia met her death when she collided with an ashtray, wielded in self-defence by Steve Owen. She'd smashed him over the head with a bottle, and was strangling him with his tie, so you couldn't really blame him.

Ethel Skinner, 2000

When Ethel returned to Albert Square with inoperable cancer, she decided that she did not want to die in a hospice, and had been hoarding morphine tablets against the day when she could no longer live with dignity. Dot was persuaded, against her better nature, to ease her passage, and Ethel died on the night of her 86th birthday.

Ashley Cotton, 2001

This was the crime for which Dot could never forgive her son. Poor, misled Ashley was out to 'get' Mark Fowler for what he'd done to his dad – only to find that Mark's bike, which he was riding in a revenge frenzy, had no brakes.

Steve Owen, 2002

After he had got away with murder in 1999, Steve's days were numbered. Matthew Rose nearly rid the world of him, but it was left to Phil to drive Steve to his death during an exciting car chase. Luckily, baby Louise (who was also in the car) escaped unscathed.

Harry Slater, 2002

Dirty Uncle Harry dropped dead of a heart attack in Spain, after his nasty little secret had become public property. He was universally unmourned.

Angie Watts, 2002

Sharon returned to Walford to bury her mother who had died, not of a heart attack as she wished the world to believe, but of cirrhosis of the liver, after a lifetime of heavy drinking finally caught up with her.

Trevor and Tom, 2002

A double death occurred when the deranged Trevor set fire to the Slaters' house, and fireman Tom went in to try to rescue him.

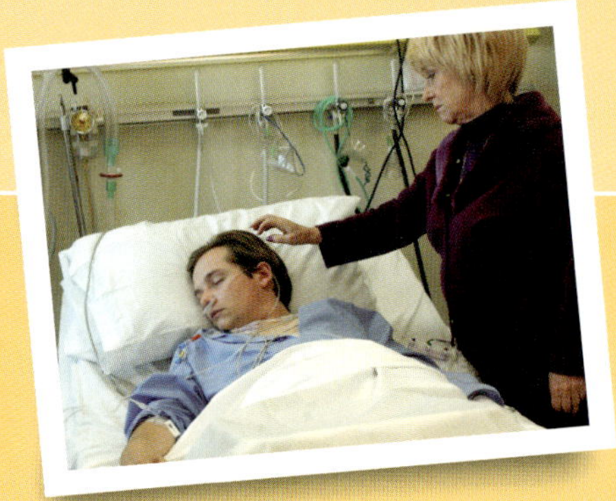

Jamie Mitchell, 2002

The dangerous streets of Walford claimed another victim when Jamie was hit by a distracted Martin Fowler. Jamie was taken to hospital, and died on Christmas Day from massive internal injuries.

Roy Evans, 2003

Roy always had a dicky heart, so it came as no surprise when yet another family drama (this time concerning Barry's broken marriage) sent him over the edge.

Jack Dalton, 2003

Dennis Rickman had got himself into very hot water with the king of the *EastEnders* gangsters, and the only way out appeared to be murder. This he achieved after much hesitation and gun waving, thus doing the entire community a great favour.

Barry Evans, 2004

The newly married Barry was having a little altercation with his unblushing bride Janine on a clifftop in Scotland... and then, suddenly, he found himself at the bottom of the cliff, very much dead, with a very merry widow.

Mark Fowler, 2004

After years of being HIV positive, Mark finally succumbed in April 2004, away from the Square, as he had always intended. He left in 2003, as he couldn't stand being a burden to Pauline. His death blew a hole in the Fowler family, from which they are still recovering.

Laura Beale, 2004

Thrown out by Ian, she was bringing up his child as Garry's – but then, after a furious row with Janine, she slipped on a toy and plunged down the stairs to her death.

Paul Trueman, 2004

Bad boy Paul tried so hard to be good, but after nearly marrying toxic Janine he slipped back into old habits and got caught up in a drugs bust. Some very angry, very powerful dealers took care of him at Christmas.

And some that got away:

▷ Angie Watts, failed suicide, 1986 ▷ Den Watts, not murdered by the canal in 1989 ▷ Dot, survived Nick's attempts to poison her, 1990 ▷ Aidan, survived jumping off a tower, 1993 ▷ Michelle, shot in the Vic siege, 1994 ▷ Ian Beale, whom Cindy's hitman missed in 1996 ▷ Phil Mitchell, who survived Lisa's murder attempts in 2001 and 2003 ▷ Kat, recovered from slashing her wrists in 2001 ▷ Trevor Morgan, despite Little Mo's best endeavours, 2001 ▷ Matt, Janine's crazy punter, survived a suicide attempt, 2002 ▷Vicki, almost died in the fire at Angie's Den in 2004 but was rescued by the man who set it alight, Billy...

Moments before Tiffany is knocked down by Frank...while Grant makes a run for it with Courtney

Tiffany and Grant

It is a truth universally acknowledged – well, in the postal district of E20 at any rate – that when two young people get together and have a child, one of them is certain to try to kill the other before too long. And so it came to pass in 1998 that Grant almost murdered Tiffany by pushing her down the stairs of the Queen Vic – or, at least, she was happy to let the world believe that he had done so. The truth, of course, wasn't quite as simple as that.

Tiffany and Grant's year started with a tentative truce; she was living with him at the pub again, despite Bianca's dire warnings. Even by Mitchell standards, this was a short-lived calm: by April Grant was getting handy with his fists again, and this time it was his own mother, Peggy, who came in for a slapping. Grant realised that he'd better make himself scarce, and went to Cyprus for a while. When he returned in June there was a new woman to push around – none other than Louise, Tiffany's mother, who had turned up expressly to cause her family maximum distress. Grant took one look at his mother-in-law and instantly decided, like you do, that he had to have her.

Tiffany, meanwhile, was making a decent attempt to carve out some form of independence. She realised that she could never really trust Grant; seeing him belt Peggy seemed to take the bloom off their romance, and she found comfort instead by going away on a massage course, taking Coutney with her. While she was away, Grant decided he really ought to get to know his wife's family a bit better, and wasted no time at all in getting his tongue down Louise's throat. It might have ended there – but when Tiffany returned, looking fabulous, announcing her determination to divorce and (worst of all) dating Beppe Di Marco, Grant reacted as any man would do in his situation, by having sex with the mother-in-law.

This little bombshell lay, unexploded, just beneath the surface of Walford life for a few months. But the truth came out, as these things tend to do, thanks to an innocent baby intercom, over which

Tiffany heard Grant and Louise discussing their illicit passion. She immediately started packing her bags, and returned to the Vic only to confront Grant one last time. They argued, there was a tussle and Tiffany plunged down the stairs, landing in hospital with a bloodclot on the brain.

Everyone thought Grant had pushed her, and he did little to persuade anyone of his innocence by attacking Beppe Di Marco by his unconscious wife's bedside, knocking out her ventilator in the process. Tiffany finally recovered, and told Grant that she was going to let the police believe he had pushed her – even though they both knew perfectly well that he hadn't. Grant was arrested on Boxing Day for attempted murder, then released on bail. Tiffany came round to the Vic for one final gloat before leaving for Spain, they tussled once again, and Tiffany was knocked down by Frank Butcher in a car. She would not live to see 1999.

Cindy and Ian

One of *EastEnders*' longest-running *mésalliances* finally came to an end in 1998, with the death of yet another well-liked female character. Cindy and Ian were at daggers drawn at the beginning of the year; she'd got off charges of abducting the children, and had managed to blacken Ian's name in the process. Then she won custody of the children – and when Ian complained, he was done for contempt of court and spent a night in the cells. When Cindy announced that she was expecting another child, this time with her posh new boyfriend Nick, Ian decided that enough was enough and that he would find out what really happened when he was shot.

A little digging turned up John the hitman, currently serving time for murder in Wandsworth, and he admitted that Cindy was his client. She was promptly banged up on remand, but the trial was delayed until after she had given birth. That was one trial that would never happen, because, when Cindy went into labour in prison in November, she died of a bloodclot on the lung. Yes, 1998 really was the year of the bloodclot.

Ian, of course, got the children back – but there was one more than he bargained for, in the shape of Cindy's new daughter. He eventually palmed her off on Gina, Cindy's sister, who instantly proved that she was unfit for such a responsible job by finding Ian attractive. Nevertheless, the baby – named Cindy, after its mother – started a new life in Devon.

Kathy and Alex

When Alex's bishop found out that he was going at it hammer and tongs with Kathy, he offered him a stark choice: the woman or your job. Alex professed his willingness to give up the cloth and start a new life with Kathy – but for Kathy this was the last straw. Phil was desperate to get her back, and, in a surprise move, even Grant weighed in with an offer of undying love and a new start in life. Confused by so many options, Kathy decided that the best thing for her and Ben was to move to South Africa, where her brother Ted was now living. She departed in April, leaving her various admirers desperate and lonely; by November we learned that she had met someone new and was planning to get married.

Terry and Irene

Separately, the Hills and the Raymonds were disastrous, dysfunctional families. Joined together, as they were by Terry and Irene's distasteful romance, they were unbearable. This didn't stop the shady couple from planning a May wedding; Irene, presumably, was swayed by the fact that Terry had just had a substantial win on the horses.

Things didn't go quite according to plan, however, when a mysterious woman hanging around at the back of the church announced mid-service that she was already Mrs Terry Raymond, and that there had been no divorce. Thus we welcomed Tiffany and Simon's mother back into their lives. Terry and Irene, undeterred, decided to go off on their planned honeymoon in any case, just not as man and wife.

EVERYONE TALKED ABOUT…

The Di Marcos

La familia Di Marco landed with an almighty thud in January, turning out in force for the funeral of patriarch Giuseppe, an old 'business' associate of George Palmer. The exact nature of the business was hard to fathom, but it was clearly shady, and before you knew it Albert Square was crawling with mean-looking men in trenchcoats wanting to have quiet talks with any Palmer or Di Marco that they could lay their hands on. This didn't stop Rosa, Giuseppe's widow, from opening up a restaurant, while her children, Gianni, Beppe and Teresa, attempted to have sex with every single person in Walford.

Gianni tried it on with Annie Palmer, but that never got very far because it soon emerged that they were probably brother and sister (Rosa and George had always been good friends…). Beppe, a policeman, turned his attentions to Tiffany, for whom

The Di Marcos – Beppe (Michael Greco), Teresa (Leila Birch) and Gianni (Marc Bannerman)

The death of Tiffany

1998 was not a good year for Tiffany Mitchell. Her brute of a husband slapped her around, pushed her down the stairs and nearly killed her in the process – and all this while she was trying to raise their child. Finally, it all became too much for her, and she prepared to move to Spain, leaving Grant to face attempted murder charges. But fate had other plans for Tiffany – thus leaving Martine McCutcheon free to have hit records in 1999.

Death drives a black car – with Frank Butcher at the wheel. Tiffany hits the bonnet while Grant stops in his tracks

Once again, Grant gives us his very best 'oh my God, my wife is dead' expression

Frank's remorse seems a little more genuine than Grant's grief

Tiffany dies as she lived – her make-up immaculate, not a hair out of place

You're never too old to fall in love: Peggy (Barbara Windsor) and Frank get cosy

he developed an obsessive, chivalric passion that involved a lot of scowling at Grant. Teresa tried to date Tony, but when she found him snogging his ex-boyfriend Simon, she began to wonder if he was really right for her.

Peggy, Frank, Roy and Pat

The erotic roundabout of Walford's senior lovebirds continued to spin at ever-increasing velocity. Peggy and Frank became more than just good friends at the beginning of the year, which should have set Roy's mind at rest. But when nosy Barry saw Pat coming out of Frank's flat one morning, he decided to spread an ugly rumour around the Square – which did nothing for Roy's crumbling self-esteem. Poor Roy had just lost his business; losing his wife was too much to contemplate, and he almost threw himself off a tall building. It was Frank who talked him down, and talked him into going into business together; Pat and Peggy found it harder to bury the hatchet, and took to slapping each other in public. The year ended with a truce. Roy was with Pat, Peggy was with Frank…but it wouldn't last.

Jamie Mitchell (Jack Ryder)

Nigel Bates (Paul Bradley), Clare (Gemma Bissix) and Julie (Karen Henthorn)

Also…

▶ Phil's godson Jamie arrives in the Square, on the run from his violent uncle Billy… ▶ Mark and Ruth fall out over the question of fostering, she has an affair with Conor and they split up for good… ▶ Dot returns to the Square £15,000 richer after an inheritance; Nick is hot on her heels, claiming to have Aids but actually on the run from the police… ▶ Gita goes missing, and Sanjay is suspected by the police of having murdered her. She later returns from a long absence with an illegitimate child… ▶ Nigel finds love with Julie, and they move to Scotland… ▶ Simon's open relationship with Chris crumbles on a boating holiday in Norfolk… ▶ Bianca gets pregnant again, and gives birth to Liam in the Queen Vic on Christmas Day… ▶ Alex's sister Melanie turns up and seems to be attracted to Ian…

1999

Steve (Martin Kemp) after murdering Saskia (Deborah Sheridan-Taylor) as Matthew (Joe Absolom) looks on

The Murder of Saskia

EastEnders' best-ever murder story unravelled with horrifying speed in the early part of 1999. It all started so innocently. Steve Owen was a slick, magnetic businessman who took over George Palmer's old club and rechristened it the e20. Matthew Rose was a bright, ambitious DJ who latched on to Steve as a kind of father figure. (His own father, Michael Rose, was a dead loss.) In the run-up to the opening of the club, Steve and Matthew became good friends, confidants, but nothing more.

And then Saskia arrived. Saskia was an old flame of Steve's, with a screw or two loose. She'd carried his child, then terminated the pregnancy after he dumped her; when she turned up in Walford, she was determined to get her revenge. This she did by coming between Steve and his new girlfriend Melanie, the vicar's sister. When Saskia managed to manoeuvre Steve into bed, she made sure everyone – especially Mel – knew about it.

Things came to a head in more ways than one on the Valentine's Night opening of the e20 club. Saskia turned up and announced to Steve that she was going to do everything in her power to make his life hell, and to that end she started knocking him around. Matthew, who was in the wrong place at the wrong time, tried to intervene. Steve grabbed the nearest inanimate object – an ashtray on the coffee table – and, in self-defence, bashed Saskia round the head with it. Saskia, spiteful to the last, dropped dead from the blow.

Panic set in. Matthew pleaded with Steve to go to the police, but Steve, being an *EastEnders* villain, wanted nothing to do with the forces of law and order, and decided instead to bury Saskia's body in a shallow grave in Epping Forest. Somehow he managed to rope Matthew in to helping him, thus implicating him as an accessory to the crime. And, just to make matters even more complicated, the entire murderous farce had been captured on the club's CCTV security cameras.

As the investigation into Saskia's disappearance intensified, Matthew started to crack. Steve stalked him round the alleyways of Walford, fixing him with his steely blue eyes every time Matthew felt an urge to confess; their *tête à têtes* became so frequent and so intense that eyebrows were raised among the Square's more knowing residents. Matthew wrestled with his conscience, but for some reason he decided not to go straight to the police with the security video, which he'd managed to steal, allowing it instead to a) fall into the hands of burglars and b) once retrieved, get wiped.

Finally, after a few false alarms, Saskia's body was discovered by some unfortunate children playing in Epping Forest. Matthew went on the run with Teresa (by now his girlfriend) and ended up in Nottingham, where he confessed everything, thus neatly making Teresa an accessory to the crime as well.

By June, both Matthew and Steve were in prison awaiting trial for murder. Nobody – least of all the viewing public – could quite believe it when Steve walked free, and Matthew was found guilty of manslaughter and sent down for seven years.

Aftermath of Tiffany's Death

Everyone in Albert Square seemed to blame everyone else for the death of Tiffany, but the real row was between Grant and Frank, who took to hovering around the Vic grunting at each other like a pair of bull elephant seals. Only Bianca knew the truth: she'd been given a letter from Tiffany that exonerated Grant for pushing her down the stairs. But Bianca was never the forgiving sort, and instead of handing the letter over to the proper authorities she gave it to Beppe, who proved to be a very improper policeman indeed when he burnt the letter and dropped Grant in it.

A verdict of accidental death was returned on Tiffany's final accident, while the CPS dropped charges against Grant for the stair incident once it came to light that Beppe had destroyed evidence. And so Walford tried to move on after the death of one of its most loved characters. Tiff's brother Simon underwent a spectacular nervous breakdown, kidnapped Courtney and nearly chucked her off a cliff, then set light to his own flat, but, that aside, things were soon back to normal…

Ian and Melanie

Why would an attractive, ambitious and intelligent woman like Melanie Healy fall for a charmless weed like Ian Beale? That was the question everyone – not least Melanie herself – was asking themselves in 1999. And yet, this improbable relationship was kindled at Peggy and Frank's spring wedding; she was on the rebound from Steve Owen, and so perhaps her judgement was clouded.

How does he do it? Ian with Melanie (Tamzin Outhwaite)

By May they were not only living together and working together – Mel and Ian were sleeping together as well, and planning to get married. Kathy turned up on a visit from South Africa to warn Mel that if she hurt Ian, she'd have her to contend with – but this made little difference to headstrong Melanie, for whom any kind of resistance usually served to encourage her.

No sooner had Melanie agreed to Ian's plans for a spectacular Millennium wedding than she found herself alone in Brighton with Steve Owen, fresh out of prison and positively reeking of criminal glamour. Naturally she slept with him, and suddenly marriage to Ian Beale seemed to lose some of its appeal. But when Ian discovered that his six-year-old daughter Lucy was ill with suspected lymphoma, Mel decided that she couldn't just walk out on her new family, and decided to stay, if only to be a mother to that poor dying girl.

And so began the countdown to the Millennium. In a rare moment of decency, Mel realised that she was entering into holy matrimony for all the wrong reasons, and tried to tell Ian as much – but he, knowing full well that Mel was trying to leave him, told her that Lucy's biopsy results were bad and that the child was dying. Even Mel couldn't argue with that, and so the New Year's Eve marriage went ahead – only for Mel to find out the truth within minutes of saying 'I do'. There was nothing wrong with Lucy apart from having Ian as a father, and Mel had been bamboozled into marriage by a wicked lie.

As the old century faded away, so did Ian Beale's second marriage – the shortest ever in *EastEnders* history.

Irene and Troy

After a failed first attempt when Irene discovered that her husband-to-be was still legally married, Irene finally tied the knot with Terry in January and looked forward to living happily ever after. She quickly discovered, however, that Terry was not only unattractive and boring, he was also extremely controlling as well – and so she set about reinventing herself as an independent woman of a certain age. She tried t'ai chi and herbal infusions, but what really did the trick for Irene was having sex, regularly and secretively, with a man half her age.

The lad in question was a handsome cad called Troy, an old friend of Tony's with a taste for – shall we say? – ripe fruit. Troy charmed his way into lodging with Terry and Irene and soon took to lurking around the house in his Y-fronts, while Irene simmered. Her resistance crumbled in November, and for a few blissful weeks they were at it like teenagers. Irene's hackles rose, however, when she caught Troy flirting with another of Walford's mature lovelies, Rosa Di Marco. When Terry finally discovered the truth on Christmas Day, Troy fled with a bleeding nose and a few unkind words about Irene's age. Terry and Irene saw in the new century hopelessly estranged.

Dan, Carol and Bianca

Bianca was pleased when her mother Carol returned to the Square announcing that she'd finished with Alan and found herself a new boyfriend. She was less than thrilled, however, when said boyfriend turned out to be one Dan Sullivan, with whom Bianca had enjoyed an underage fling some years ago. At first, Bianca tried to talk Dan into doing the decent thing and leaving immediately; when this didn't work, she did what anyone would do under the circumstances, and started having sex with her mother's boyfriend instead.

Addicted to their dangerous liaison, Bianca and Dan became extraordinarily indiscreet, rushing off to empty buildings at the drop of a hat, while their respective partners scratched their heads and wondered what was wrong. When Carol announced the happy news that she was expecting Dan's baby, Bianca flipped. Carol soon figured out what was wrong (it's never a good idea to leave incriminating photographs lying around, even if you have ripped them into four pieces), and there was the inevitable

Like mother, like daughter: Bianca and Carol (Lindsey Coulson)

exchange of recriminations and slaps. Bianca confessed all to Ricky, who immediately threw her out; Carol, meanwhile, guzzled a bottle of vodka and a fistful of pills, before rushing straight off to the hospital to terminate her pregnancy.

Bianca, for whom the whole situation was just too embarrassing, decided to take up a place at Manchester University, whither she was last seen departing with baby Liam. Ricky, despite last-minute jitters, did not accompany her.

Grant's Departure

Grant was at a bit of a loose end after driving his wife to an early grave. He mooched around the Square looking lost, and had an affair with Nina, which ended when he discovered she was an ex-prostitute. Bored and restless, he tried to destroy his mother's marriage, ousted his own mother-in-law and former lover from the Square, beat up a social worker who was concerned about Courtney, and even accidentally visited a gay bar. Finally he decided that there was only one thing left that he hadn't yet done: he must sleep with his own brother's wife, presumably in a delayed revenge for Sharongate. So, when Kathy came back for a brief visit in September, he seduced her.

Phil found out, of course, but chose not to confront his brother until they were at the wheel of a speeding car trying to escape from a successful robbery. Phil started shooting at the dashboard, the

EVERYONE TALKED ABOUT...

The St Valentine's Night Massacre

EastEnders has a special way of celebrating the big festivals. Christmas, of course, is usually marked by something especially juicy – but in 1999 it was the turn of Valentine's Day to get the full Walford treatment. Steve Owen's demented ex-girlfriend Saskia had been stalking him for some time, but she chose the opening of the e20 club (on 14 February, natch) to turn into a murderous hellcat. Unfortunately for her, Steve got a bit handy with the self-defence, and she ended up in a shallow grave in Epping Forest.

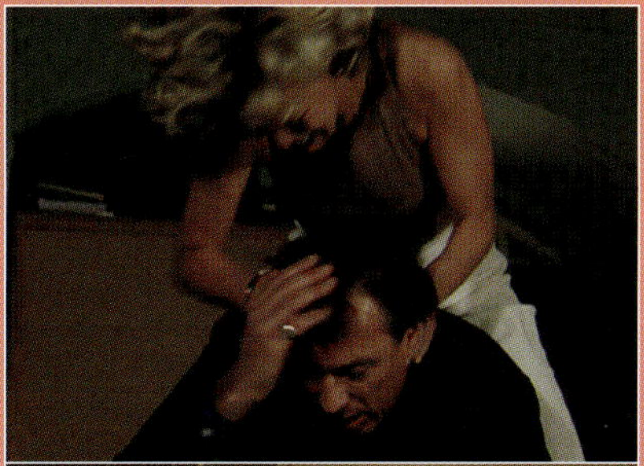

Having coshed Steve over the head, plucky Saskia attempts to strangle him

Steve reaches out for the first object that comes to hand, while the unfortunate Matthew witnesses it all

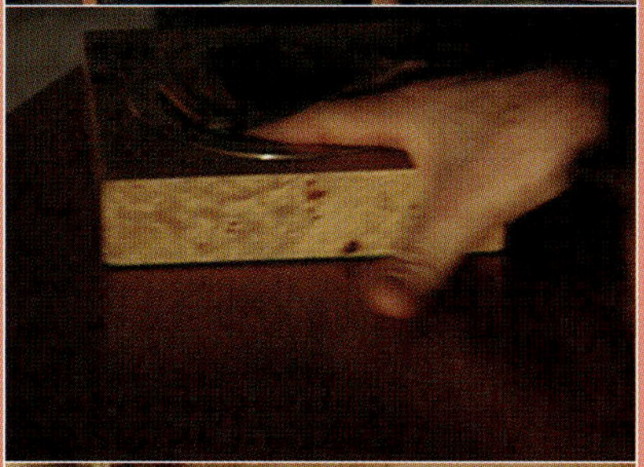

Et voilà! The fatal ashtray, lovingly rendered in harmless foam rubber by the Elstree props department

Another one bites the dust, as Saskia joins the show's spectacular death toll

Grant and Courtney bound for Rio

car crashed into the Thames, Phil bobbed to the surface…but Grant was nowhere to be seen. The money turned up in a holdall addressed to Phil, while Grant was last seen on a plane bound for Rio, clutching the hapless Courtney in his burly arms. And that was the last we saw of Grant – to date.

Also…

▶ A new doctor, Fred Fonseca, arrives at the surgery and reveals that he's gay… ▶ Irene's niece Nina, a former prostitute, is stalked by a former client… ▶ Lisa has an affair with Michael Rose, but later transfers her affections to Phil… ▶ Ruth discovers that she is pregnant with Conor's baby, and leaves… ▶ Recovering from his breakdown, Simon goes off travelling with Tony… ▶ Peggy's cancer returns and she has a mastectomy… ▶ Roy buys black-market Viagra in an attempt to have a sex life with Pat… ▶ Barry starts going out with Natalie, and they're married on New Year's Eve… ▶ Janine seduces Jamie, and claims to be pregnant so Frank will let her stay in Walford…

Barry and Natalie (Lucy Speed)

Dangerous to Know

Everyone loves a villain - not least the women of Walford, who have always found the whiff of criminality absolutely irresistible.

Den Watts

Back in the day, he was the last word in smooth-talking naughtiness, and however horrible he was to his wife, daughter and mistress, somehow we forgave him. He was the ultimate East End bad boy, and when he returned to the square more than a decade later, he set pulses racing all over again. However, for all his tough talk and tougher action, Den soon proved to be a coward when dealing with the really hard decisions in life – flunking all his family responsibilities, and always taking the path of least resistance (where many have been willing to follow). Will there ever be a villain quite like him again?

Grant Mitchell

Grant was little more than a thug, but somehow he brought out the mothering instinct in otherwise sane women. Perhaps it was that baby face, those big blue eyes... or perhaps it was the fact that he was so clearly damaged goods, a latent psycho who had been pushed over the edge by his experiences in the Falklands. Whatever the reason, women flocked to him, and Grant could never resist. But as soon as he married them (Sharon, Tiffany) he started using them as punchbags, and either drove them away or drove them to their deaths. He currently resides in Rio with daughter Courtney – poor girl.

Phil Mitchell

Another much-married Mitchell brother who, by rights, ought to be banged up for life, considering his form. Whatever comes in his way, he either beats it up or burns it down: he's a one-man crime wave, and thus, naturally, irresistible to women. Otherwise intelligent women like Kathy, Lisa, Kate and Sharon have all put up with the stink of stale booze, the permanent stubble and the shiftiness – but never for long.

Steve Owen

Possibly the best-looking, certainly the best-dressed man ever to stalk the mean streets of Walford, Steve Owen was nevertheless utterly unscrupulous when it came to crime. He stole, dealt drugs, took drugs and, of course, accidentally-on-purpose murdered his pesky ex, Saskia. He lied in court, he philandered his way around the Square, and he met a just but messy end. Blame the mother, Barbara, a quasi-incestuous lush; Steve practically danced on her grave when she died.

David Wicks

Pat's suave son slunk into town on the run from some very dodgy underage sex allegations, and immediately started sniffing round the indecently young Bianca, who turned out to be his own daughter. Despite this Freudian nightmare, David was irresistible to women – particularly Cindy, who threw away her marriage to Ian Beale for a few stolen moments in the Portacabin with Dishy Dave.

Simon Wicks

With his blow-dried hair, rolled-up jacket sleeves and toothy grin, Simon 'Wicksy' Wicks was the apotheosis of 80s manhood. He went through the women of Walford like a dose of salts, but at the end of the day Slippery Simon was a bolter, and left Cindy high and dry and, quite literally, holding the baby.

Andy Hunter

Andy is a crook, a blackmailer, a gangster and a bully, and as such he has half the women of Walford running around after him. Kat paid dearly for jilting him at the altar, then Sam rushed in like a lamb to the slaughter. He's also got plenty of muscle to back up his tough reputation as there's never a shortage of thick-headed brutes willing to do his dirty work.

Also:

▷ Dennis Rickman, after coming out of prison he seduced nearly every woman on the Square and murdered Jack Dalton, the rascal
▷ Dan Sullivan, who had two generations of Jacksons on the go
▷ Paul Trueman, a man with connections

The worm turns: Matthew made Steve's life hell in 2000

Matthew's Revenge

The final act of the Saskia story was played out in the e20 club – the very place where the unfortunate ashtray did its work in 1999. After just a year in prison, Matthew had changed; when he reappeared in Walford, he was no longer the sweet boy who had dated Sarah Hills. No: the 2000-model Matthew was a wild-eyed psycho who terrorised Steve Owen and claimed to have made some 'tasty' friends on the inside. He daubed 'DEAD MAN WALKING' around Steve's door, blocked his toilet, strewed his path with broken glass – and then went really nutty. In February, Matthew captured Steve in the e20 office and embarked on the most extreme psychotic episode ever witnessed in *EastEnders*.

He tied Steve to a chair, scared him into believing that he had murdered Claudia and framed him for it, then doused the office with petrol and started playing with a lighter. Hardman Owen was soon a grovelling, gibbering wreck, and Matthew realised that he'd got what he wanted: power. The fact that Claudia was alive and well, and that the 'petrol' was only water, were by the by; Matthew had the upper hand, and ran cackling into the Walford night, never to be seen again.

Steve was a broken man. He hit the bottle, and when that was empty he hit the coke. Things could only get worse, and Steve reached his nadir when he became Billy Mitchell's twitching, pleading drug slave. Steve wisely quit the Square in June, leaving his dignity behind him.

Phil and Lisa

Lisa's dogged devotion to the foul Phil Mitchell was one of *EastEnders*' least plausible love stories. She was introduced as a gutsy, fun-loving biker chick – and yet, the moment she fell for Phil, she morphed into a cringing spaniel of a woman, always creeping back for another beating. Throughout 2000 she yo-yoed between Mark (who loved her with equally canine devotion) and Phil, who treated her mean to keep her keen. When Lisa discovered she was

Blondes have more fun: a rare disagreement in the Vic

pregnant, Phil turfed her out, but not before suggesting she should run along to the abortion clinic. This was enough to make Lisa realise that she really, truly loved Phil and wanted to bear his child.

After much mooching and cringeing around the Square, Lisa and Phil decided to play happy families in April – just in time for her to miscarry. Phil responded by shouting abuse at her, but when he realised the gravity of the situation, he was, for once, supportive and took Lisa away for a few days to recover.

Frank and Pat

That ol' devil called love reared its ugly head again when Frank realised that, after all, it was Pat he loved and not Peggy. His timing couldn't have been much worse. Peggy had just got over a mastectomy, and had undergone reconstructive surgery, partially to please Frank; she was feeling so positive she even wanted to renew her marriage vows. Frank naturally interpreted this as a signal to start making up to his ex-wife, and when by chance Walford's senior lovebirds went on holiday to Spain, the stage was set for a fast-moving bedroom farce.

While Terry and Irene were busy splitting up, and Peggy and Roy wandered around liked blissed-out zombies, Pat and Frank succumbed to the romance of Spain by rolling around in bed like a pair of out-of-control teenagers. Pat tried to cool it on their return to London (despite Frank's crafty attempt to manoeuvre them both into the plane's loos), but when Frank turned up on her doorstep naked apart from a comedy bow-tie, she realised that this thing was stronger than both of them.

Like all guilty lovers in Walford, they started trysting in the car lot Portacabin, where they were nearly rumbled by Peggy. It was then that comedy turned to tragedy: Peggy realised her marriage was a sham, Roy acted like a recently poleaxed bull, and even Pat started to think that, after all, Frank was just too dodgy to plan a future with. They tried to elope to Manchester together, the romantic fools, but got cold feet half way up the motorway and turned back to face the music. This involved Peggy reading out Frank's 'Dear John' letter in front of the entire pub, and a great deal of traditional cockney slapping.

Phil offered to have Frank 'rubbed out', but Peggy declined, and threw him out instead. Pat missed her lift and ended the year as an Untouchable, ekeing out a miserable existence as a cleaner at the B&B, while Peggy flipped out at Christmas (when else?) and smashed up the pub with a baseball bat.

Sonia and Jamie

At the other end of the age scale, Sonia and Jamie were 'just good friends' at the start of the year, both smarting from recent unsatisfactory sexual encounters. Jamie lost his honour to Janine (who then told everyone he was 'rubbish'); Sonia, depressed and drunk, accidentally had sex with Martin, who promptly dumped her.

After a rocky summer, in which neither could speak a civil word to the other, Sonia and Jamie finally allowed love to triumph in August, and, not long after, planned a romantic evening in which they would seal their relationship in a mature, adult way. But like all the best-laid plans, this night of love went badly awry. Sonia, who had been worrying for weeks about her weight, locked herself in the toilet with severe stomach cramps. Jamie, thinking she'd bottled it, went off in a testosterone-fuelled huff, leaving poor Sonia to scream the house down. Fortunately for her, the Slater women were on hand. They pushed past the confused Jamie and immediately realised that this was more than just trapped wind: Sonia was having a baby. And, yes, it was nine months, almost to the day, since her drink-sodden fling with Martin Fowler...

Sonia was in shock, and for the first few days of motherhood she couldn't even pick the baby up. Jamie fled, feeling that he'd been taken for a ride. Eventually, after much agonising soul-searching, Sonia decided to put the baby – whom she named Chloe – up for adoption.

The aftermath of Sonia's unplanned pregancy was devastating. It looked as if her relationship with Jamie would never recover, although by the end of the year they were at least 'mates' again. And when the truth about the baby's father leaked out, Pauline did what any loving grandmother would do: she marched across the Square and slapped Sonia in the face.

The Death of Ethel

Ethel Skinner turned up unexpectedly on Pauline's doorstep in July, announcing that she'd come for a long stay. It soon emerged that she was dying; cancer had spread to her brain, and it was only a matter of time before she was reduced to being, in her words, 'a thing in a chair'. This she could not bear, and she pleaded with Dot to ease her passage, when the time came, by administering a stash of morphine tablets that Ethel had been carefully squirreling away for just that purpose.

Dot was torn between her strong Christian principles and her love for Ethel, who played shamelessly on their long friendship and, eventually, won her battle one dark night in September.

Ethel's death destroyed Dot. Desperate with grief and guilt, she gave herself up to the police, demanding to be punished – but the police, with no

Ethel gets a proper Walford send-off

evidence, would not press charges. So Dot took to shoplifting, and when that didn't get her banged up, she smashed up the pharmacy. Even that only netted her a fine, and so she added contempt of court to her growing charge sheet and spent two harrowing weeks in prison.

Goodbye, Di Marcos...

Nobody really knew what to do with the Di Marco family, who had been languishing in the pizza restaurant without a decent storyline between them. There was a flurry of interest in Beppe, when his ex-wife Sandra turned up in Albert Square and started trying to take their son Joe away with her, but, despite an endless on/off romance between the former lovers, the story came to naught. More satisfying was the plight of brother Gianni, who started going out with Steve Owen's sister Jackie, only to find that, when the moon was right, she became crazed and violent with PMT. Gianni spent much of the year getting kicked, punched and scratched; when Jackie left in July, he turned his attentions to a female bodypiercer called Raylene.

Little Nicky Di Marco made a bid for attention by claiming to have been sexually assaulted by her teacher Rod; this prompted a flurry of chest-beating from her brothers, but again the storyline fizzled out when charges were dropped. Finally, there was nothing else for it: the Di Marcos would have to go. All of them, bar Beppe, moved to Leicester in August; it was as if they'd never been.

...Hello, Slaters

The Di Marcos' place was taken by the Slater family, who arrived in Walford like a soap within a soap, so complex were their inter-relations. Mum was dead, Dad was grieving, Nan was fencing stolen meat, daughter Lynne was in danger of losing her fiancé to

The Slater family arrives – Garry (Ricky Groves), Lynne (Elaine Lordan), Charlie (Derek Martin), Zoe (Michelle Ryan), Little Mo (Kacey Ainsworth), Kat (Jessie Wallace)

sister Kat, Little Mo was getting beaten up by her rotten husband Trevor and as for Zoe...well, we'd have to wait for a while to learn about Zoe. The advent of the Slater women was like a dose of Viagra to the men of Albert Square; never had there been such universal preening and posing among Walford's male population, nor such seething among the clan's females.

Seducing the nanny – Ian with Laura (Hannah Waterman)

Also...

▶ Ian recovers rapidly from his failed marriage and starts sexually exploiting his new nanny, Laura... ▶ Beppe nearly dies after accidentally taking a dose of amphetamines... ▶ Terry attempts to seduce Mel... ▶ Mark gets ill when he stops taking his medication... ▶ An unexploded Second World War bomb is discovered in nearby Victoria Road... ▶ Roy and Phil are rumbled doing a roaring trade in stolen cars... ▶ Ricky gets depressed, smashes up a car and then disappears in the cab of a lorry headed for France... ▶ Nick Cotton and his son Ashley turn up to persecute Dot...▶ Jeff proposes to Pauline in the Vic, where she publicly humiliates him... ▶ Steve wants to marry Mel... ▶ Ian's plans to become a property magnate misfire, leaving him bankrupt... ▶ Irene dumps Terry in Spain and drives off into the sunset... ▶ Terry returns to Walford alone and is instantly befriended by Janine... ▶ Phil and Mel have sex on Christmas Day...

EVERYONE TALKED ABOUT...

Sonia's baby joy

It was the date from hell. Sonia and Jamie had been going out, on and off, for months, and decided to cement their relationship with a romantic night in. But Sonia, who didn't actually realise she was pregnant after a brief encounter with Martin Fowler, went into labour on the bathroom floor, which is guaranteed to ruin even the best date. The response to this storyline was electrifying, and the BBC set up a special helpline to advise young women who also found themselves in Sonia's situation.

▶ Jamie fails to notice that his girlfriend is going into labour, and prepares to leave in a huff

▶ Slaters to the rescue! Mo and Little Mo get Sonia down to the living room where they manage to deliver...

▶ Chloe! But this is one arrival that will bring only misery to everyone in Albert Square

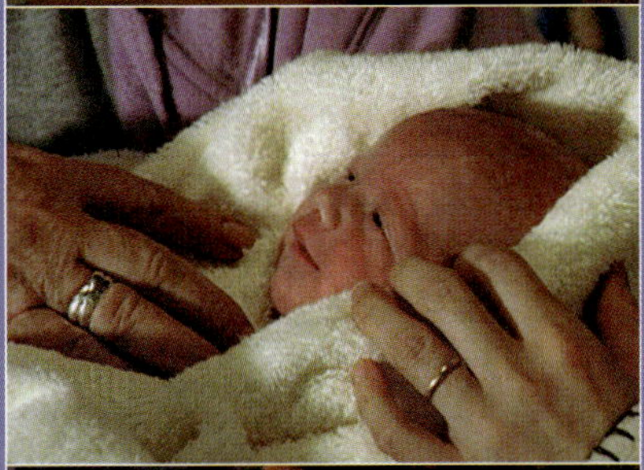

▶ Sonia faces up to motherhood

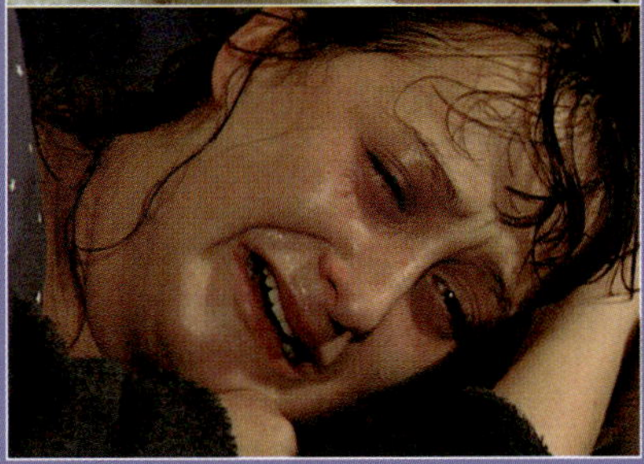

Todays SPECIALS
FRENCH ONION
40
TODAY
40
TODAY
PHILIPS
2

Behind the Scenes

Location and Studios

As we all know, Walford is situated somewhere north of that loop of the River Thames that forms the Isle of Dogs. And yet, in another reality, Walford exists a few yards off the high street of a suburb of north London, and is little more than a cluster of ugly office blocks, warehouses and fake buildings. Elstree Studios – once the home of the British film industry, more recently home to *The Muppet Show* and *Top of the Pops* – is the real, bricks-and-mortar location where the virtual reality of *EastEnders* is created.

Walking from Elstree and Borehamwood train station up an unremarkable suburban shopping street, you'd never guess that you were anywhere near the hub of the biggest show on British television. Nothing advertises the studios' presence; there are no road signs pointing the way, no *EastEnders*-themed pubs or restaurants in the vicinity. The first sign that something unusual might be going on is the presence, in all weathers, of a small gaggle of teenage girls on a quiet street corner that leads to the studio security gate. They're there to catch a glimpse of their favourite soap stars as they travel to and from work. Anyone approaching the studio, by car or even on foot, is subject to their scrutiny. Generally speaking, they're no trouble, and they keep warm even on bitter winter days with Thermos flasks of tea and coffee.

The main gate to BBC Elstree (top) and one of the useful milk floats (above) on the lot

The bricks look solid; the pub looks very much like a pub. But, of course, this is an illusion.

Inside the complex there's a curious mixture of mundane reality and total fantasy. The Elstree complex is shared with another major BBC production, *Holby City*, so for a start you're likely to see actors from either show strolling between studio or lot. Every so often you'll see a milk float parked up outside a building, bearing the unnerving logo of the 'Walford Dairy' (they are actually used for ferrying people and things around the lot; they have the great advantage of being silent). But, those clues aside, it's still hard to believe that anything interesting goes on in what looks like a slightly forlorn light industrial estate. Even the show's most ardent supporters would agree that Elstree isn't the most beautiful spot on God's earth.

Penetrate the inner sanctum, however, and all is revealed. The heart of Elstree, and the part which is most carefully guarded against unwanted intrusion, is the Albert Square lot – that odd mix of real, solid buildings and fake fronts that make up the familiar location for so much of *EastEnders*' outdoor action. It's easy, once you're in it, to forget that this is not a real London square: the grass, the trees, the pavements and the roads are all genuine enough. The bricks look solid; the pub looks very much like a pub. But, of course, this is an illusion. Push open the door of the Vic and all you'll find is a vestigial corner of the bar (which can be seen from outside) with a few ice buckets on it and...not much else. Look at the houses from the end of the terrace, and you'll realise that they're all front – literally. Realistic facades, made largely of wood and render, are propped up on a framework of timber; these are houses with no interiors.

The gardens in the centre of Albert Square are the place where reality and fiction blend in the strangest way. The iron railings, for instance, look solid enough – but they're only made of plastic and won't support the weight of a man leaning against them. The trees and bushes are growing nicely, but sometimes

Mother Nature needs a bit of help. Because the show is filmed six weeks in advance of transmission, seasonal changes have to be faked. False daffodils are stuck into the grass to hasten spring, while leaves have to be stuck on to naturally bare branches. In the autumn, leaves sometimes have to be stripped to give an illusion of winter. If you ever see Christmas decorations around the Square, you can be certain that you're looking at scenes that were filmed in late October or early November.

Practically all the exterior scenes that you see in *EastEnders* are filmed somewhere on the Elstree lot; it's much easier to adapt an existing available space than to go to the trouble and expense of taking the cast and crew outside. So, for instance, certain small parts of Walford Cemetery have been created on the backlot; it's much easier to stick up a little gravestone on an unused patch of grass than to ship everyone out to North Watford Cemetery, which is used for big funeral scenes. Car chases and other big street scenes have to be filmed outside, of course – but these are kept to a minimum, as they're hugely demanding in terms of scheduling time. They're also a potential nightmare for security – because, wherever *EastEnders* goes, the press is bound to follow, and there are no lengths to which they will not go in order to scoop a hot storyline.

When it comes to interiors, the production moves away from the familiar Albert Square lot and into Elstree's massive studios. The enormous Stage One is home to some of the most famous sets, notably the interior of the Queen Vic and some of the major family homes. The pub, particularly, is strange, a brightly lit space surrounded by the darkness of the studio, in which a vast team of cameramen, directors, make-up artists and technicians scurry. It's possible to walk straight out of the pub and into someone's front room; the big sound stages are a maze of oddly juxtaposed environments. Spaces formed between different sets become impromptu

HM The Queen visits the Square, 18 November 2001

props stores, or are used by the actors to rest or refresh their make-up between takes.

However realistic these interiors look – and they do, right down to the wallpaper in a sitting room or the pint mugs gleaming above the bar – there are constant reminders that this is not life as we know it. Look closely at the pumps in the Vic, for instance, and you'll find Ashtons Premium Ales, Jenkins Leading Lager, Eagle Eye Lager. The fags are just as fake as the booze; Walfordians smoke Final Draws or White Lites, neither brand being available in your local tobacconist. They eat Hank's Spicy Chilli Crisps, they read the *Walford Gazette*, or *Sasha* magazine (for young women) or *Geezer!* (for the lads).

As *EastEnders* has expanded over the years, from two weekly episodes to four, it's taken over more and more of the Elstree site – which, fortunately, is big enough to accommodate the expansion. But it remains an enclosed world, carefully guarded, access to which is granted to few outside the immediate production. The help desk is constantly being asked by callers if they can book a tour of Albert Square, or hire out the Vic for a function (answer to both questions: no). The press is rarely invited on to the lot, although plenty have tried to come in anyway – most notably a tabloid journalist who went to the absurd lengths of joining an extras agency and getting a job on *EastEnders*, just so that he could file his story. (He was detected, and booted out.) Sometimes – for a variety special that went out on Christmas Eve 2003, for instance – the gates are thrown open to an invited audience of local people, competition winners and friends of the cast, but even they are carefully vetted and chaperoned during their time in Walford. Other than that, visitors are few. Sick children are sometimes given a pass, as are royalty; the Queen and the Duke of Edinburgh made a memorable trip in November 2001. They watched the filming of a scene in the Vic (a fake scene was specially written; there were far too many press around to risk leaking a real storyline). They went on a lightning tour of the lot, and were introduced to the cast (Michael Greco greeted the Duke of Edinburgh with a cheery ''Ello, mate!'). Security helicopters buzzed above Elstree for the duration of the visit, making any filming impossible – but they'd gone after two hours.

It was certainly a historic day for *EastEnders*, and for Elstree. But, lest anyone get too big-headed about it, let us remember how Prince Philip reacted when asked if he and the Queen watched the show at home. 'We turned it on once,' he replied, 'but there was a lot of shouting, so we turned over.' So much for royal patronage. Camilla, however, is a fan.

You may think you know your way round Albert Square, but did you know:

- **The war memorial in the gardens features the names of several well-known Walford families – as well as the names of many people who have worked on *EastEnders***
- **The BBC canteen at Elstree is often pressed into use as Walford Hospital; it's just a question of changing the signs**
- **The *EastEnders* lot was previously used as the German building site in *Auf Wiedersehen, Pet*. This was knocked down in order to build Albert Square**
- **A plaque on the bench in the garden reads: 'Arthur Fowler – he loved this place.' Another plaque, never seen on screen, commemorates a former executive producer, and reads: 'John Yorke – he loved this place'**
- **Studio C at Elstree, which now houses various interior sets, used to be home to *Top of the Pops***
- **Three webcams around the lot transmit live images to the *EastEnders* website. They're turned off if a sensitive storyline is being filmed, although there have been mistakes. When Tiffany's funeral was being shot, someone forgot to turn off the webcams – despite strict secrecy about her death!**
- **Filming had to be suspended in 2002 when part of the railway bridge – which is only made of wood – blew down**
- **Every time you see a tube train go over the viaduct, it's going in the same direction. And it's not real; the train is 'painted' on in post-production**

If the cameras are to turn over at 8.15 in the morning, that usually means that actors need to arrive at the studio with an hour to spare for make-up and costume.

Acting

A job on *EastEnders* may seem like a dream for many an aspiring actor – and it's true that nothing gives you a higher profile than working on a popular soap. The rewards are good, too; while not in the Hollywood league, they'll buy you a very comfortable lifestyle indeed, with plenty to spare.

But the reality of working on a four-times-a-week drama is far from glamorous. Once an actor signs up to a job on *EastEnders*, he or she is handing control of life over to the production. In soap, scheduling is king, and there's little room for manoeuvre. The actors have to do what they're told, when they're told, and if they don't, they will damage not only their own careers but also the smooth running of the entire show.

Generally speaking, *EastEnders* is filmed five days a week, Monday to Friday, with Saturdays always available for catching up or to film big, intensive blocks of scenes that feature one particular group. New actors have an annual holiday allowance of two weeks, which they can take only when the storylines allow; that goes up to four weeks for artists who have been with the show for over five years. They also have a guaranteed fortnight off over Christmas, when the entire production shuts down by virtue of 'triple-banking' – a system whereby an additional production team records a week's worth of episodes as well as the eight episodes in production, often on a foreign location (that explains those trips to Spain, Scotland or Clacton). It's a way of storing them up to allow everyone to take some time off with their families and friends.

The working day starts early, and can often finish late. If the cameras are to turn over at 8.15 in the morning, that usually means that actors need to arrive at the studio with an hour to spare for make-up and costume. Twelve-hour days are not unusual,

Shane Richie, for instance, had to appear in practically every scene shot in the Vic when Alfie was the landlord, in order to lend authenticity to his working life.

especially for those actors who are heavily involved in a high-profile storyline. But you don't even need to be the centre of attention to have a big workload; Shane Richie, for instance, had to appear in practically every scene shot in the Vic when Alfie was the landlord, in order to lend authenticity to his working life. He may not have had any lines, but he had to be there behind the bar, pulling pints and chatting to customers, day in, day out. To compensate for this, Alfie was rarely seen out on the lot during his tenure of the Vic.

When the show added an extra episode and went out four times a week in 2001, the production schedule was radically overhauled in order to allow for increased productivity. Now there are always two production teams working at Elstree at any one time, shooting different blocks of episodes – and an actor frequently has to bounce between one team and another. This can lead to some very strange continuity problems; it's not unheard of for an actor to film a few scenes leading up to his death, then film the death itself, then bounce back from beyond the grave to film more scenes from the run-up.

Because of the high volume of material that's produced by each team – they create something like 13 minutes of film each, per day, which is far higher than the TV average – and because of the paramount importance of good continuity, it's vital that the whole *EastEnders* production is run by a very strong schedule. And it's in this respect that the actors have to surrender much of their private life to the dictates of the show. Because time is so tight, there is very little room for manoeuvre if an actor wants time off for, say, a dentist's appointment or a parents' evening. Sometimes personal requests can be accommodated by the company manager, who liaises between the actors and the schedulers, so that rotas can be changed to allow an actor to attend a wedding or such like. But this kind of flexibility, while not uncommon, is far from guaranteed.

'Some actors take to that better than others,' says Carolyn Weinstein, *EastEnders*' company manager. 'It's all to do with personality. There are some actors who completely understand that the schedule is ruled, and they just bow to it and get on with things; in a sense, I think they quite like having their life run for them. But there are others who find it very hard. You can tell them over and over again that the schedule can't be changed to accommodate their social diary, and they'll still get upset. And it's not just the younger, less experienced actors who feel that way. It's something that I've seen right across the board.'

Sometimes, however, even a schedule as tight as this has to make allowances for sudden, unforeseen circumstances. If an actor is ill, or suffers a bereavement, for instance, he or she would not be expected to work, and filming has to carry on around their absence. With a permanent company of between 45 and 50 actors, a lot of things can go wrong. Patsy Palmer once fell ill right in the middle of filming a big Bianca storyline; the schedule had to be radically altered in order to accommodate her absence, and the scripts were rewritten so that the character's personal dramas were talked about rather than seen. In 2002, both Barbara Windsor and Kim Medcalf were involved in car accidents, necessitating a short recovery leave; again, schedules were changed at the last minute to cover for them. In a real crisis, if a central character is unable to work for whatever reason, all leave is cancelled and the rest of the cast has to step into the breach.

Fortunately for the sanity of all concerned, these crises are rare, and the schedule works well. It should do; when the programme added its extra episode in 2001, there had already been a thorough feasibility study to ensure that the team wasn't biting off more than it could chew. In *EastEnders*, scheduling comes before everything: a plan of

In *EastEnders*, scheduling comes before everything: a plan of availability is worked out for actors, studio, lot and location well in advance of the writers getting to work on actual episodes.

availability is worked out for actors, studio, lot and location well in advance of the writers getting to work on actual episodes; it's then their responsibility not to write anything that's going to be impossible to film.

The volume of material that has to be produced by *EastEnders* hasn't just affected the organisational side of the show; it's also had a huge effect on the way that the actors work. When there were only two episodes a week, the actors would spend full days rehearsing their scenes. They no longer have that luxury. With the schedule being so tight, and two full teams demanding the actors' time, they have to go straight into each scene with a small amount of rehearsal directly beforehand – all of which is scheduled in. As a result, it's important that all the actors have a very instinctive approach to their characters; it's no good coming to a part in *EastEnders* if you have to spend a long time preparing or 'getting into character'.

'It is cast now in a way that takes full advantage of the artists' own personalities,' says Louise Berridge, former executive producer. 'In the past, the writers would create a character on paper, and then we'd go out looking for an actor who would be able to embody that creation. Now this process has been turned round; they look at the actors first, and find people that they think will bring something interesting to the show. They put them into workshops, and weed out the ones that don't suit, and are left with a pool of actors who bring a ready-made character to the show. We started doing that when we introduced the Slater family, and it worked very well. All the strong actors in the workshops were women, and so from that we developed the idea of a family dominated by strong female characters, which is what the Slaters became. The characters of Kat, Lynne, Little Mo and Big Mo were all absolutely dictated by what the actresses brought to the workshop.'

Alfie, Nana and Spencer Moon in the kitchen

The Miller family – causing havoc around the Square

'It's very different from any other type of acting because you have to know exactly what the character would do in any situation.'

The same technique has been used to cast the Moons and, more recently, the Millers. 'It saves the writers a lot of time and energy,' says series consultant Tony Jordan. 'As soon as we've found the right actors, we send tapes of them to the writers, so they've got a face and a voice in their minds when they start writing for those characters. It means, I think, that the characters seem more real and vivid. Anything that we may have lost in terms of rehearsal time has been more than made up for in this new way of developing characters out of the strengths of the actors' personality.'

This means that, more than ever, the *EastEnders* cast have to 'become' the characters that they're playing. 'It's a question of delivering the best-quality performance you're capable of at the speed that's demanded,' says Steve McFadden (Phil Mitchell). 'It's very different from any other type of acting because you have to know exactly what the character would do in any situation. I came from drama school, where we were always taught to ask why a character was doing something, what he was thinking, what was behind his actions. There's no time for that on *EastEnders*. When they say go, you go! You have to deliver. So you have to develop a sixth sense of what the character is like, and you inhabit that character completely. Some people find it quite hard to let go, especially when they've been shooting an intense storyline.'

Over the years, the production team has learned that working to such a high standard, and at such a rate, can be very hard for actors – and they need a bit of looking after as a result. The biggest disaster for the show would be if the actors developed a high burn-out rate, therefore it's important to give them adequate breaks and make sure that any problems are addressed before they affect the show. 'We tell all the new artists coming on to the show that they're going to lose control of their life to some extent,' says company manager Carolyn Weinstein.

'And we talk to them about how to survive the pressure. It's not just the pressure of work – all our actors are now under intense scrutiny by the press. It's really changed over the last five years, as the spotlight has moved on to the actors' private life.

'I always advise them to think very carefully before they allow the press to get hold of anything on them at all. If you sell your wedding, or your baby, or your home to a magazine for a lot of money, you can't very well start asking for your privacy back when it all goes wrong for you. My advice is never make yourself vulnerable to the press. If you don't want them to get pictures of you falling out of a nightclub at three in the morning paralytic drunk, then don't do it! Live your life with some control and dignity – because once you lose control, you can be certain that the press will be there to capture it. There's always a certain amount of intrusion, whether you ask for it or not – but if you don't give them anything, they'll leave you alone. We do as much damage limitation as we can, but ultimately the actors have a responsibility as well. They're responsible for how they live their life off the set, and they're responsible for maintaining the public image of the show. It's a tightrope, especially for the younger ones. They can suddenly be in a position of having a bit of money and a lot of fame, and some of them run wild – it's only natural, and I'd do the same. We just try to steer them through it as best we can. We have a duty of care towards the entire cast, particularly the young ones. Their parents are putting them in our hands, and we have to be responsible for them.'

This parochial care extends to the actors' professional life as well. Any work that they choose to do outside *EastEnders* is carefully regulated by the production team in order to avoid conflicts of interests. Actors are not, for instance, allowed to appear in any commercials while they're under contract, nor can they take acting jobs outside the

Ross Kemp left EastEnders *to seek wider small-screen stardom*

Very few have established themselves as major stars in their own right, entirely independently of *EastEnders*.

BBC (the days of panto with current *EastEnders* stars are long gone). Many of the actors do private charity work, which also has to be cleared by the production. 'That sounds mean,' says Weinstein, 'but it has to be understood that the actors are doing it as private individuals, not on behalf of the show. The show has to maintain an impartiality; if we openly supported one charity, that would be unfair. That doesn't mean we stop actors from doing charity work – in fact, loads of them do it. Christopher Parker (Spencer Moon) has run the marathon for a well-known children's charity, and Charlie Brooks (Janine Evans) did it for a cancer charity. A lot of them visit kids in hospital. But it's not something we publicise as an *EastEnders* initiative.'

Given the nature of the business nowadays, it's hard to know whether actors will stay with the show for more than a few years. Contracts are shorter, and the temptation for an actor who's made a big splash in *EastEnders* to move into other areas of TV or film is great. Whenever an actor decides to leave the show, he or she is offered a range of options – and, in the majority of cases, it suits them to have an 'open door' back into the show at a future date. If that's not what's wanted, the next best option is to be killed off: it provides an actor with a spectacular storyline with which to launch a post-*EastEnders* career. Sometimes, however, if the production team feels that a character or family isn't working out, they simply move, and are never heard of again. That, unsurprisingly, is the least popular option.

For actors who have left the show, whether temporarily or for good, the challenge of building a career after *EastEnders* is enormous. Some have sunk without a trace, after a high-profile departure; it's hard, sometimes, to shake off the character with which millions of people associate you. Others have enjoyed some success outside the show for a few years, and have been able to dip back in and out of Albert Square when it suits them. Only a very few

Life after Walford

It's not always easy being an ex-*EastEnder* – but some have done better than others.

The Big Four

Only four ex-*EastEnders* have enjoyed success that eclipsed their original soap fame. **Nick Berry** had a brief pop career, then hit the big time in *Heartbeat* and *In Deep*. **Michelle Collins** had major success with *Sunburn*, *Real Women* and *Two Thousand Acres of Sky*, as well as dozens of single films. **Martine McCutcheon** managed to find real success as a recording artist, stage star (*My Fair Lady*) and film actress (*Love, Actually*). **Tamzin Outhwaite** held her own in *Red Cap*, *Out of Control*, *Final Demand* and *Frances Tuesday*.

Never out of Work

Not quite in the premiere league, but doing very well indeed. **Paul Nicholls** went into uniform for *City Central*, then proved his acting skills in *The Passion*, *Canterbury Tales*, *A Thing Called Love* and a handful of feature films. **Ross Kemp** went on to a series of starring roles on ITV – although not always finding the success he'd hoped for. **Martin Kemp** also skipped to a lucrative ITV deal, but has yet to find the right vehicle. **Joe Absolom** has worked consistently in shows like *Servants*, *POW*, *The Long Firm* and *Doc Martin*, and **Lindsey Coulson** has continued her career in *Clocking Off*, *Paradise Heights*, *Manchild* and *The Stretford Wives*.

Straight into *The Bill*

Ex-*EastEnders* who still want a regular wage are welcome to apply at Sun Hill police station where **Russell Floyd**, **Roberta Taylor** and **Todd Carty** have become popular mainstays.

Could Try Harder

Among those who have enjoyed sporadic success in the acting profession are **Michael French**, who starred for a while in *Holby City*; **Gillian Taylforth**, who appeared in *Messiah* before *Footballers' Wives* came along; and **Patsy Palmer**, who needs to find another starring vehicle after *McCready and Daughter*.

All Change

EastEnders seems to have put some actors off TV for life. **Anita Dobson** gave it all up for a career on the stage (and being Mrs Brian May); **Michelle Gayle** put her energies into her ongoing singing career; and, in the most dramatic change of all, **Michael Cashman** went into politics, lobbied for lesbian and gay rights and became an MEP.

You won't find these brands in your local shop

have established themselves as major stars in their own right, entirely independently of *EastEnders*. It's a hard act to follow – and, with the workload associated with the show, a hard act to maintain over a long period. So next time you're standing on the corner outside Elstree Studios, huddled around your Thermos and envying the glamorous lifestyle of those actors who sweep past you in their chauffeured cars, think again. Life as an actor on *EastEnders* is hard, hard work.

Costumes, Make-up and Props

Close your eyes for a moment and think of *EastEnders*. What do you see? Chances are it's something like Pauline's beige jumper, or Dot's red hair, or Pat's earrings. Perhaps you see the ashtray with which Steve dispatched Saskia, or the iron with which Little Mo flattened Trevor. Or maybe your first image is of Kat's leopard-skin tops and industrial quantities of eyeshadow…

The visual aspect of *EastEnders* is the responsibility of an army of artists and technicians who work behind the scenes to make sure that the characters and their surroundings look memorable, believable and consistent. And that's no mean feat when you consider the number of characters who have passed through Albert Square, the many changes that they have gone through and the constant possibility of their return. Who would have believed, before 2003, that Den Watts would come back to Walford after apparently dying in the canal in 1989? And yet, for all those years, the *EastEnders* props and costume department kept certain key items of jewellery, and Den's passport, just in case…

The props store at Elstree is a real-life Aladdin's Cave. It's a huge hangar of a building, in which every conceivable space from floor to ceiling is taken up with a bizarre collection of items of all sizes, from large

The props store at Elstree is a real-life Aladdin's Cave.

things like suitcases and bits of furniture, right down to pens, boxes of matches and rings. If a character is seen leaving the Square carrying a certain piece of luggage, it's important that he or she be seen returning with the same piece – even if several years have elapsed. And even for characters who haven't left, props have to be kept in strict order. Every person in the cast has their own filing cabinet drawer and a plastic wallet containing things like keys, wallets, purses, mobile phones, letters, photographs – all the little bits and pieces that make up a person's identity, just as much as hairdos and make-up.

Wandering around the *EastEnders* props store can become a positively macabre experience. There's a corner that's affectionately known as 'Death Row', which contains coffins, caskets of ashes, gravestones and other morbid paraphernalia; you never know when a character is going to have to visit the cemetery, and it's important that the correct gravestone can be whipped out, dusted off and re-erected. Of course, they're not real – they'd weigh far too much, and are made of wood or polystyrene.

Seemingly innocent items can also have a sinister significance to those who know the show well. Little Mo's almost-fatal iron forms part of a 'black museum' – and, like the famous e20 ashtray, it's moulded out of foam rubber and painted to resemble the real thing without actually endangering the life of the actor into contact with whom it came. On a more wholesome note, there's always a lot of food around the props store. Most of it is real: the fruit and veg that's seen on the market stall, for instance, or the stuff that's served up in the café. Only one item is regularly faked, and that's fish for the fish stall: try putting real fish out in the sun and under lights for a day, and you'll realise why.

While the props store is downright surreal, the costume store is more like a cross between a fashion museum and a giant shop. Here you'll find rail after rail of clothes, each belonging to an individual character. Outfits are put together from these 'wardrobes', just as you would match an outfit at home, and it's important that each wardrobe reflects the tastes and status of the character. 'We try hard to dress the characters as they really would dress in real life,' says series costume designer Di Humphreys. 'Nearly everything comes from high-street shops or charity shops. There is nothing expensive or designer here, unless a storyline really calls for it.'

Continuity photos, personal effects and possessions are filed for every character

Clothes have to reflect personality, but also a character's socio-economic position.

EastEnders isn't *Dynasty*, and so the costume budget remains low, the styles relatively downbeat. Older actors know their characters so well that they have a clear sense of what exactly they should, and should not, wear. June Brown, for instance, is most insistent that Dot would only ever wear clothes from charity shops – and so the costume team scours local second-hand outlets to find the right sort of coats, blouses, skirts, hats and jewellery that meet with Ms Brown's approval. Pam St Clement (Pat) has a collection of some 125 pairs of earrings, and is a dab hand at picking out exactly which pair will match (or, more often, mismatch) an outfit.

Clothes are a way of telling a story, just as much as words or actions. If a character is down on his luck, his clothes will reflect it. If someone is becoming more confident or successful, their dress sense will improve as well. Sonia, for instance, went through a metamorphosis in 2003, lost weight, improved her clothes – and caught the eye of Martin Fowler as a result. Sam Mitchell's wardrobe has reflected her evolution from empty-headed bimbo to aspirational businesswoman. And then of course there's Janine, who memorably set fire to her prostitute outfits during a fit of remorse, and later emerged as a svelte, deadly schemer.

When a new character comes into the show, the costume designers will develop a look for them based not only on the writers' and directors' ideas of the character, but also on what the actors think will work for them. When the Ferreiras came into the Square in 2003, Ronny and Tariq were presented as being club kids, heavily influenced by the styles and tastes of their own music-dominated environment. Vicki Fowler arrived as a rebellious, somewhat punky character, but has since mellowed to a fashion-conscious high-street girl. Alfie Moon's taste for flamboyant shirts expressed his outgoing, larger-than-life character.

'I have to do most of the shopping for the actors,' says Di Humphreys, 'and so I buy huge amounts of stuff. I do most of it in Milton Keynes, which is near where I live, and at first they thought I was a mad woman, buying 50 pieces in a day and then taking half of them back. I've had to explain what I'm doing to a few of the shops, and now they understand and they're always happy to help.'

Clothes have to reflect personality, but also a character's socio-economic position. Kat, for instance, would love nothing better than to wear expensive designer gear – but, given her relatively lowly status, she's forced to wear cheap knock-offs. 'Jessie Wallace is a great sport; she'll wear anything I give to her, no matter how tight and outrageous and cheap it is. In real life she's a very good dresser, she wears a lot of beautiful vintage stuff or just very simple jeans and sweaters, but she lets me put her into some hideous stuff.' And whatever the costume department chooses, you can be certain that the viewing public will be taking note. 'I had a letter a while ago saying that Lynne Slater would never be able to afford the top I'd put her into,' says Humphreys. 'I had to write back saying that the top came from the high street, that Lynne was a woman in her 30s with a job and a husband and it wasn't unreasonable for her to be able to dress like that.'

The costume department isn't just responsible for getting the look right – they also have to ensure that the actors are comfortable and that the clothes are properly cared for. As *EastEnders* is shot six weeks before transmission, the real weather conditions don't always suit those that are being portrayed on screen. April episodes, for instance, might be shot in February – and there's a world of difference between a balmy spring and a bitter winter. So, while the

Pam St Clement, Barbara Windsor and Jessie Wallace add the final touches in the make-up department

There are three teams of three make-up artists servicing the entire *EastEnders* production at any one time.

actors rehearse their lines, they're well wrapped in enormous parka coats that bear the word 'COSTUME' on the back in white paint. These are whipped off just in time for the take – but even then, most of the actors are dressed in thermal underwear.

When clothes have been worn for a certain amount of time, of course, they have to be washed – and that means that extreme care has to be taken to get the right garments back on to the right rails. Each item of clothing is labelled with the character's name inside – and that label stays there for as long as the garment is still needed. When the costume store starts bursting at the seams, however, Humphreys and her team hold a jumble sale. 'They're very popular events,' she says. 'The entire cast and crew comes to pick things up. My prices are very reasonable; you can get a nice jumper for about £2, for instance, and it'll still have its label in it. Each of those garments has a little bit of *EastEnders* history about it.'

Make-up is more important to some characters than others. Phil Mitchell, Dennis Watts and Martin Fowler, for instance, rarely appear on screen wearing anything more than a very light tinted moisturiser, a bit of concealer under the eyes if the actor has had a late night, and, when occasion demands, black eyes, blood and bruises. But for some of the most memorable *EastEnders*, make-up is just as much part of them as the accent or the name.

There are three teams of three make-up artists servicing the entire *EastEnders* production at any one time. They're responsible for getting the characters prepared from one scene to the next within a very tight schedule – often having only five minutes before an actor has to be whipped away to film a new scene. 'It's harder than it sounds,' says Elizabeth Armistead, series make-up designer, 'because sometimes they're filming completely different episodes and we only have the shortest

Before EastEnders *Jessie Wallace made her living as a make-up artist*

Steve McFadden having some make up applied before filming

'Most actors can cry on demand, but no actor in the world can keep that up for the time it takes to shoot a scene in *EastEnders*.'

time to do the change. If it's meant to be a different day, then I'd probably just change the lipstick, because it's very easy to wipe that off, tidy the mouth up and then put a different colour on. The eyes, however, are a very different business, especially for characters like Kat or Sharon who wear a lot of eye make-up. I wouldn't touch the eyes unless I had to, because they take so much more time. You'll probably notice, if you look really carefully, that those characters have exactly the same eyes on different days of the week, because we haven't had the time to redo it all.'

The real challenges for the make-up department come when characters have to go through traumatic experiences – which, this being *EastEnders*, is pretty frequent. It's easy enough to make a character look rough: just don't put any make-up on them at all, and the cameras will do the rest. The effect can be startling, especially for some of the actresses who usually do their faces quite carefully. 'It's all to do with interpretation of the script,' says Armistead. 'I have to judge just how much make-up to take off in order to achieve the right degree of roughness. Some of the artists are more willing to take off make-up than others. I've had a few of them begging me for a little bit of blusher, or a little bit of eyeliner – but they always understand that telling the story comes first. I can usually talk them round by saying, "Well, in this scene you're at your lowest ebb, but in the next scene we'll be able to give you a bit more make-up to suggest that you're recovering, and then soon you'll be in full warpaint again."'

If a scene requires a lot of crying, that means extra work for the make-up department. 'Most actors can cry on demand, but no actor in the world can keep that up for the time it takes to shoot a scene in *EastEnders*. You have to help them. We have a very useful little thing called a tearstick, which is basically a menthol cone on a stick, like a lipstick, that you can apply at the top of the cheekbone or near the lower eyelid. The menthol fumes stimulate the tear gland to produce tears, and you're in business. It's easy to use if an actor is supposed to be crying at the top of a scene, because the make-up artist can just nip in and apply it. But if they have to start crying in the middle of a scene, it's harder. The more experienced ones know how to do it themselves: they'll rub a bit of tearstick on to their finger and thumb at the start of the scene, and then when they're about to have to start crying you'll see the hand going up to the face. That's when they rub the tearstick on around the eyes, and the tears start flowing. I always look at the scripts in advance, and if there's a lot of big, emotional scenes coming up, I order in half a dozen extra tearsticks.'

Getting the tears to flow isn't that hard, then – but patching up the damage afterwards, as everyone knows, isn't so easy. 'If an actor has to go straight from a big crying scene into a normal scene, we have to take action to calm their eyes down. Sometimes we only have five minutes. First of all, I sit the actor down and talk to them, try to get them to relax. Then I use a bit of moisturiser to wipe off any remaining tearstick, and to clean up make-up that may have run. Then I put in some eyedrops to knock back the redness, and apply cold, wet cotton wool balls to reduce puffiness. I remember once when Lucy Benjamin (Lisa) left the show for the first time, and she had to do about 18 crying scenes in one day, then go straight into a perfectly normal, calm scene. It took us a bit more than five minutes to calm her eyes down, but we did it.'

Each actor's make-up design is carefully controlled by the department in order to ensure that it doesn't vary too much from one episode to another. 'When a new actor comes in, I meet them and talk to them about the kind of look they're going to have. Then, if necessary, I'll take them to one of my favourite salons in London to give them the right haircut. Then we'll talk about the kind of make-up they like to use, what they're allergic to, any brands they prefer, and I'll go out and do my shopping based on that. Each character then has a make-up bag that follows them around the set. Nigel [Harman, who plays Dennis] uses very little, because he's got very good skin and doesn't need much. I gave him a sharp, spiky, sexy haircut because it was important to convey that aspect of the character, so we maintain that with a bit of product, and that's it.'

Other characters, however, have bigger make-up bags. 'Sharon and Kat have the biggest at the moment,' says Armistead, 'because both of those characters like to put on a face for the world. Jessie does her eyes and lips herself as she used to be a make-up artist before she became an actress, and she can do it very quickly and professionally, which suits me. Letitia [Dean, who plays Sharon] tends to do her own hair and make-up as well, although sometimes she'll just come in and say, "Oh, I'm tired. Please do it for me."'

Older characters tend to need more time in the make-up artist's chair, in order to achieve the right degree of haggardness. 'Probably the longest make-up job is Dot Branning. June [Brown] wears a wig for the role now; for years and years she used her own hair, but I think she just got sick of having to dye it all the time, and so now she has a wig. But she hates it! She hates the glue, and having to wait for it to dry, and is always complaining about how uncomfortable it is. June's a very good sport, though – and it's got to be better than actually having to do that to yourself…'

Special occasions call for special make-up designs – and nothing stretches the department's resources more than one of *EastEnders*' regular conflagrations. 'We've become quite good at doing fires, because there have been so many of them. It's all to do with soot, sweat and heat burns.

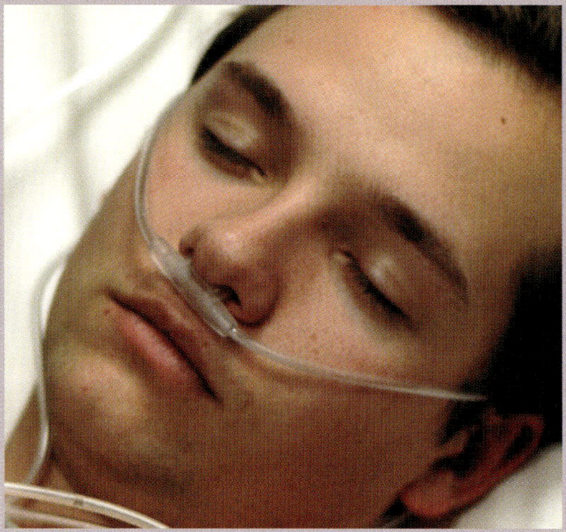

'When Jamie was dying after being knocked over by a car, there were no injuries to see, because all the damage was internal.'

We have consultants from the fire brigade who come in and tell us if we're doing too much or too little, and we've learned how to make it look really authentic by putting black round the nostrils and the tear glands and the corners of the mouth. The biggest fire job I can remember was when Tom got killed inside the Vic; we had an awful lot of people, including Sharon, looking very rough that day.'

Sickness and injury are also the responsibility of the make-up department, although there's a limit to how much they can actually show in a pre-watershed programme. 'We don't overdo the gory stuff,' says Armistead. 'We tend to suggest it rather than go into too much detail – and besides, we don't have the time to do a huge prosthetic wound, like you'd see on other dramas. What we can do quite effectively is suggest illness. When Jamie was dying after being knocked over by a car, there were no injuries to see, because all the damage was internal. But we could do a lot by breaking down his skin, making him paler, shading around his eyes. We don't want them to look silly – but you had to know that the boy was dying.'

As well as patching and painting, the make-up department provides a vital part of the actors' support network. 'Often we're the only people that they'll see in between rushing from one scene to another, and so it's very important that we can talk to them and calm them down or encourage them, whatever's needed. We're always around on the set or the lot, so the actors see a great deal of us. Most of them like being in make-up; it's a chance for them to unwind, even if only for five minutes. You learn a lot about what's going on, just from those conversations in the chair. You get them first thing in the morning, when they're sleepy and a bit vulnerable. A good make-up artist knows how to make an actor not only look good, but feel good as well.'

2001

EastEnders starts airing four times a week from August

He had it coming: but which of his legions of enemies pulled the trigger?

Who Shot Phil?

Who shot Phil Mitchell? That was the question on everyone's lips in the first half of 2001. There were just so many people who wanted him dead at that time – including a large part of the *EastEnders* audience – that, really, anyone could have done it.

The events leading up to the attempt on Phil's life stand out as one of the most outrageously complex storylines ever to grace the show. It all stemmed from that fateful Christmas Day in 2000 when Phil and Mel slept together – for no apparent reason other than to annoy everyone else. Phil instantly decided that he didn't love Lisa any more, and proceeded to make her life hell. Lisa, being the masochistic type, lapped up every cruel word, every humiliation, with a pitiful gratitude, and decided that this was the man she wanted to father her children. No sooner was the decision made than Lisa became pregnant.

Mel (who, remember, was supposed to be Lisa's best friend) got the jitters, and told Lisa that Phil was not to be trusted – and offered, as supporting evidence, the fact that she'd slept with him at Christmas. When Lisa confronted her beloved with this fact, he outgrossed himself once again, leaving Lisa with a burning desire for his death.

She wasn't the only one. Steve had also found out (on his stag night, naturally) that Mel had slept with Phil. Ian got riled when Phil boasted about having had his ex-wife and his mother. Mark was fuming over Phil's treatment of Lisa because Mark, by this stage, was hopelessly in love with her. Yes, on the night of 1 March 2001, there were plenty in the Square who wanted Phil dead.

On the night of Steve and Mel's wedding, as the happy couple were driving out of the Square, someone turned up at Phil's house and fired a bullet into him. While Phil fought for his life in hospital, the gossips of Walford decided that Steve must have been the assassin – and so, on his return from his honeymoon, he was duly picked up by the police and charged.

Set up – Dan (Craig Fairbrass)

But it was not Steve. Nor was it Ian, who had been seen lurking around the body (and had left Phil to die; nice work, Ian). It was, as we discovered when Phil got out of hospital, none other than Lisa herself, who, in a moment of madness, 'borrowed' a gun from the e20 club and went on the rampage. It did not, however, suit Phil's Machiavellian purposes to have Lisa arrested; he wanted instead to frame Dan for the deed, in revenge for taking advantage of Jamie whilst he was in hospital.

It was at this point that *EastEnders* became more complicated than *The Maltese Falcon*, as viewers tried to puzzle out why there was such a mystery over what was actually quite a simple attempted murder. Anyway, Dan got framed, Lisa and Phil called a truce (what's a little bullet between friends?) and Ian somehow got off the hook as well. Dan swore revenge, although for what exactly nobody could be too sure.

Mark *v.* Nick

There was never much love between Mark Fowler and Nick Cotton. The two of them had knocked around in dodgy racist gangs as kids, but since then their paths had diverged – and when Mark discovered that Nick was supplying drugs to his kid brother Martin, he snapped. Spiking Nick's drink, Mark led him up to the Walford viaduct and watched in horror and delight as Nick plunged to the ground.

The accident left Nick crippled and vengeful. He attempted to enlist his own son, Ashley, as the instrument of his revenge, but Ashley lost his bottle at the thought of setting fire to Mark's house and, after discovering that Nick had tried to poison Dot, ran home to his mummy. The feud simmered throughout the spring, and when Ashley returned in June, the two men were having regular pops at each other in the Square. Mark foolishly attempted to run Nick over on his motorbike, prompting Nick to sabotage the bike by draining off its brake fluid. Ashley, furious that anyone had tried to hurt his beloved daddy, commandeered the bike for a spot of revenge – and drove straight to his death.

When Dot learned of Nick's part in his own son's death, she decided that even her capacity for forgiveness had been exhausted, and she banished him to the outer darkness whence he has never, to date, returned.

Mel is Kidnapped

Dan's trial for the attempted murder of Phil finally took place in July, after the poor man had spent some months in prison. When the prosecution evidence crumbled and Dan was handed a 'not guilty' verdict, he set about sorting Phil out once and for all – but, like many before him, he found that Phil Mitchell was a tough nut to crack.

Realising that the only person Phil cared for other than himself was Mel, Dan kidnapped her in August and demanded £100,000 each from Phil and Steve for her safe return. The money was forthcoming, but when Mel discovered that Steve had been playing around behind her back, she decided that she'd rather remain kidnapped. She reached a quick deal with Dan, and disappeared with £50k of the ransom money. Dan was never seen again; Mel, however, returned to Walford and burned the e20 club to the ground.

Little Mo and Trevor

We had known for some time that Little Mo's marriage to Trevor was troubled; just how troubled became graphically apparent over the course of 2001. Mo grew worried when Trevor had not returned from a stint working away, so she and Billy tracked him down, only to discover he was living with a pregnant woman called Donna. Trevor decided that he wanted Mo back and promised to turn over a new leaf. Donna later tried to warn Mo off, telling her that Trevor had beaten her during the pregnancy, but Mo turned a deaf ear as always and toddled meekly back to face the music.

Trevor was a wily old fox. He conned everyone into believing that he'd changed his ways, that he was seeking counselling for his violent temper and that he was ready to be a good husband to Mo. No sooner were they back together, however, than he started getting handy with his fists. When he discovered that Mo was seeing her family behind his back, he flung her against the wall and cracked her head open. From that point on, Mo's life became one hellish round of beatings in private, denials in public. Trevor burnt her hand with the iron, subjected her to the most cruel mental torment and then, on the day in December when he discovered that she was planning to go to her own sister's wedding, attacked her in the bathroom and raped her.

Still, Mo remained blindly loyal to her husband, even listening to his insane suggestion that maybe they could have a child together. When Trevor found Mo's birth-control pills, he kicked her so violently in the stomach that she could no longer hide her pain from her family. But still she wouldn't leave him – and it was only when Mo discovered that Trevor had tried to come between Zoe and Kat that she saw the light and fled.

Trevor was hot on her heels. Cornering her in the Fowlers' house on New Year's Eve, where she was babysitting Louise, he attempted to terrorise her into returning home – and had another go at raping her, just for good measure. Mo picked up the nearest

Little Mo finally snaps and hits Trevor (Alex Ferns) with a handy iron

heavy object – an iron – and bashed him over the head with it. And that, surely, was the end of Trevor...

Zoe and Kat

Little Mo wasn't the only Slater sister with problems in 2001. When Kat found out that Zoe was planning to leave London to go and work for her jolly Uncle Harry in Spain, she put her foot down, much to Zoe's disgust. 'You're not my mother!' said Zoe, in typical teen defiance. But Kat had news for her: 'Oh yes I am.'

The whole sorry, sordid saga soon unfolded before a horrified public. Uncle Harry was much more than an uncle to the teenage Kat, and had been regularly having sex with her, the result being that she had conceived a child. Viv, her mother, knew the truth – but Charlie, who was kept in the dark, went along with a plan to raise the baby as their own. And so Zoe grew up unaware of the fact that the woman she called her mother was really her nan, and her sister was her mum, and her uncle was simultaneously her great uncle and her father.

Kat shows some motherly love

Little wonder, then, that Kat slashed her wrists and Zoe fled the Square, to be found some weeks later begging and filthy on the streets of London. From this life of squalor she was rescued by a scheming creature called Roxy, who put her up in a flat and attempted to lure her into prostitution. Zoe flunked her first assignation (she got so drunk on whisky she vomited over the punter) and was helped to escape from Roxy's retribution by a co-worker, Kelly. Roxy pursued her to a homeless shelter, and was about to drag her back to a fate worse than death – when in rushed the cockney cavalry, in the shape of Kat, who headbutted Roxy and took Zoe home for Christmas.

Mark and Lisa

Mark's dogged devotion to Lisa was one of Albert Square's more puzzling phenomena. She gave him little encouragement, she was in love with someone else whose baby she was carrying, she showed signs of severe emotional disturbance and she revealed herself as a would-be assassin. None of this prevented Mark from announcing to the world that Lisa's unborn child was his. Eyebrows were raised, but Mark insisted that they'd taken all the relevant precautions in relation to his HIV, and that they were going to settle down as a family. When baby Louise was born in November, it seemed like the perfect happy ending.

Despite the fact that Lisa yo-yoed from Mark's place to Phil's place on a weekly basis, Mark never wavered in his chivalry, not even when Lisa tried sleeping with him and decided that it wasn't her cup of tea. Finally, worn down by so much unswerving decency, Lisa agreed to marry Mark at the end of the year – only to have their romantic moment disturbed by Phil rushing in to see 'his' daughter. The secret (never much of a secret, as nearly everyone already knew) had finally leaked out, and Little Louise's chance of a settled home life evaporated before it had even begun.

For better, for worse: Garry and Lynne get married

Also...

▶ Pauline attempts to get custody of baby Chloe, but when Martin admits he doesn't want to be a father she backs down... ▶ Sonia and Jamie get back together again and finally have sex... ▶ Roy asks Pat for a divorce, but when she decides to emigrate to New Zealand, he relents and takes her back... ▶ Anthony Trueman has an on/off affair with Kat... ▶ Anthony's brother Paul gets into trouble with Angel and his gang... ▶ Paul and Anthony's mother Audrey dies... ▶ Janine comes between Terry and his girlfriend Margaret... ▶ Laura and Ian marry... ▶ Peggy starts going out with Harry... ▶ Peggy is obliged to sell the Vic when she discovers that Frank has dropped her in massive debt... ▶ The new owner of the Vic is revealed to be none other than Sharon... ▶ Natalie gets pregnant, but nearly has an abortion... ▶ Dot has a mental breakdown and has to go in to a home... ▶ When she comes out, Jim Branning proposes to her... ▶ Steve's poisonous mother Barbara dies... ▶ After endless delays, Garry finally marries Lynne... ▶ Sharon and Phil start going out again, to Peggy's disgust... ▶ Sharon reveals that she can't have children, after aborting Grant's baby... ▶ Janine has a brief affair with Billy, then moves in on Paul...▶ Laura nearly burns down the chip shop... ▶ Beppe gets an STD and falls in love with Lynne... ▶ Roy sees his old girlfriend Jane and meets their son, Nathan... ▶ Pauline fancies an old schoolfriend called Derek, who turns out to be gay...

EVERYONE TALKED ABOUT...

Little Mo irons Trevor

Inanimate objects have always been put to novel uses in *EastEnders*: Pauline's frying pan, Steve's ashtray, and, in 2001, Little Mo's iron, with which she nearly killed her abusive husband, Trevor. This was probably the most unpleasant scene ever shown in *EastEnders*, combining rape and attempted homicide – and, yes, it was on a day when the rest of us were trying to enjoy ourselves, New Year's Eve. The blow was not fatal – but that didn't make things any better for Little Mo, Walford's ultimate female victim.

▶ Trevor follows Little Mo into the Fowlers' kitchen, where she is attempting to take refuge, and tries to rape her

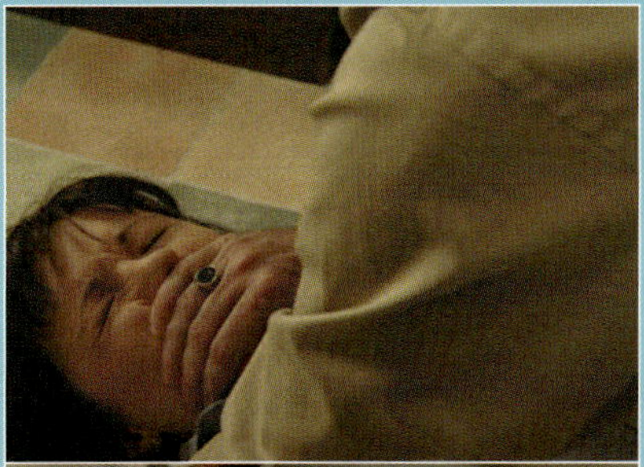

▶ And then she finds the iron, which makes satisfying contact with Trevor's head

▶ Blood on the lino: Trevor almost becomes yet another victim of the scriptwriters' homicidal tendencies

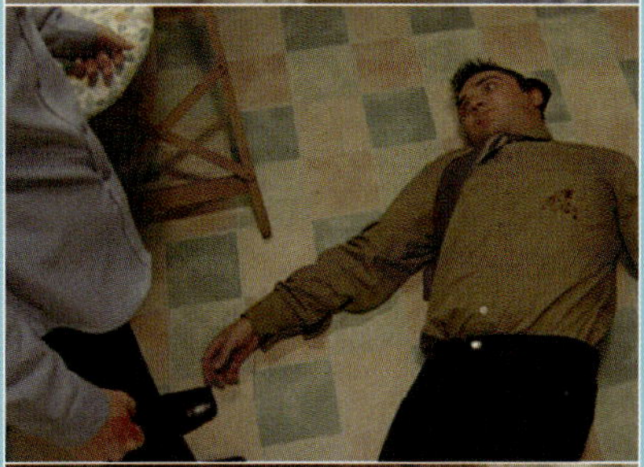

▶ Believe it or not, things will actually get worse for Little Mo in the next couple of years

Drama Queens

They're the heart and soul of *EastEnders* - strong, passionate women who go to pieces where men are concerned and always come back for more.

Kathy Mitchell (Hills, Beale)

One woman above all others has taken it on the chin in *EastEnders*, and that's Kathy. Even before we met her, she'd been raped and given the baby away for adoption. Then she was raped again, her marriage crumbled, her second marriage (to Phil) imploded, her daughter turned up and committed suicide, and she had tragic affairs with Laurie Bates, Eddie Royle, Tricky Dicky and, almost, Grant. She was regularly slapped in the face and publicly branded a slut in the Vic. To cap it all, she lived with the shame of being Ian's mother. She has earned her place in the South African sun.

Angie Watts

Angie burned through Walford like a deranged comet, trailing broken marriages and broken bottles. She thrived on drama, and was never happier than when plotting some insane revenge on Den. Destined never to be happy, she escaped to America where she drank herself slowly to death; her sodden remains are now buried in Walford Cemetery.

Sharon Watts (Mitchell)

She may only have been Angie's adopted daughter, but Sharon certainly inherited the drama-queen gene. After a troubled, drink-sodden adolescence, she emerged as an unbalanced sexpot with a fatal taste for bullies. She tried both Mitchell brothers, and found them wanting; when she returned to the Square after a long absence, however, it was straight back to Phil's bed that she raced. Now, with Dennis in her life, she'll never be bored.

Cindy Beale (Williams)

Try as she might, Cindy was never cut out to be the domestic type. She married Ian out of desperation – who else would provide for her? – but that didn't stop her from carrying on with both Wicks boys, right under Ian's nose. Attempted murder, child abduction and serial adultery did not go unpunished, and Cindy died in childbirth, in prison. Walford will not see her like again.

Pat Evans (Harris, Beale, Wicks, Butcher)

Like a spider in the middle of an enormous web, Pat is almost solely responsible for the Byzantine complexity of family relations in Walford. Practically the entire cast of *EastEnders* is related to her in some way – and if not, she's married them. After sending Roy to his premature reward, she is currently available – but who would have the nerve to take her on?

Tiffany Mitchell (Raymond)

Tiff arrived in the Square like a breath of fresh air – a cheerfully unscrupulous girl who led Bianca astray and could flirt to Olympic standard. Then she met Grant, and the die was cast. Every so often she tried to flee from the ceaseless abuse, and on her final flight she was squashed by a car. This transformed her into the Patron Saint of Walford's drama queens.

Bianca Butcher (Jackson)

During her reign as Walford's trouble-maker-in-chief, Bianca stirred up so much stink in the Square that it must have come as a relief, even to Ricky, when she left for a new life in Manchester. She wrecked his life, and her mother's (by sleeping with her boyfriend – nice touch), and she wasn't much more of a comfort to her father, with whom she shared a quasi-incestuous passion.

Kat Moon (Slater)

We knew, as soon as she arrived with her fake tan and hoop earrings, that Kat Slater meant trouble. She wasted very little time in establishing herself as a drama queen by revealing that her youngest sister, Zoe, was in fact her daughter. Then she stole her boyfriend for good measure. Alfie tamed her for a while but she couldn't be happy for long, and finished 2004 as a man-eating drunk.

Mel Owen (Healy, Beale)

Mel was a nice girl with surprisingly bad taste in men. As the vicar's sister, she should have known better than to get involved with wrong 'un Steve Owen, or to sleep with Phil Mitchell (bad move). And she certainly shouldn't have married Ian Beale, which can only be attributed to temporary insanity. She wisely dumped him minutes after the wedding.

Janine Evans (Butcher)

Janine was a true dramatic diva. After a troubled childhood (bed-wetting, running away), this ugly duckling emerged as a true swan, albeit with a ravenous appetite for cocaine and a penchant for prostitution. She hit Jamie like a truck, conned Terry and conned (and killed) Barry before finally taking the rap for a murder she didn't commit.

Also:

- ▷ Sue Osman, who broke down after the death of her son
- ▷ Sam Mitchell, who's slept with every able-bodied man in Walford
- ▷ Sonia Jackson, gymslip mother and widow at 17, now Mrs Fowler
- ▷ Michelle Fowler, a woman with a fatal taste for married men
- ▷ Louise Raymond, who seduced her own daughter's husband
- ▷ Irene Raymond, who liked 'em young

2002

Mel on the run to Portugal

Phil-Mel-Steve-Lisa-Mark

Relations between Phil, Mel, Steve, Lisa and Mark became so labyrinthine in 2002 that something had to give – and by the end of the year, at least one of the Famous Five was dead, another one missing presumed dead, a third just plain missing, and another well and truly in the departure lounge.

It all revolved around Phil, of course, with Peggy on hand as a sort of cockney Greek chorus, always ready to strike up with some helpful comment like 'Louise is a Mitchell!'. When he wasn't trying to get custody of his daughter, Phil engaged in an insane feud with Steve Owen, for reasons that neither of them could really remember, but which they dimly knew had something to do with Mel. When neither of these pastimes was enough, Phil would either sleep with Lisa, or beat Jamie to a pulp.

There were so many outrageous climaxes to this story – Phil holding Steve hostage with a couple of scissor-wielding maniacs, for instance, or Steve attempting to relocate practically the entire cast of *EastEnders* to California, that it came as some relief when, in March, Steve crashed his car – with Phil in hot pursuit. Phil snatched baby Louise from the wreckage, but left Steve behind as the car blew up.

Louise was returned to her mother, and spent the rest of the year being routinely snatched by someone or other. Lisa married Mark and then decided to rekindle her affair with Phil. Mel discovered that she didn't own the e20 club after all (Steve had sold it to Beppe just before he died), but she got arrested for drug dealing and money laundering anyway. When Mel discovered, in prison, that she was carrying Steve's baby, she was so angry with her late husband – who, she believed, had attempted to murder Phil among other crimes – that she temporarily decided to abort. Lisa, in a rare moment of sanity, confessed to Mel that actually she'd shot Phil, and so Mel – as confused as the rest of us – left Walford to go and figure it all out.

What Happened to Lisa?

That was not quite the end of the story, however. After implausibly deciding that she loved Phil and was prepared to start a new life with him, Lisa walked out on Mark and moved into the Vic. She was spared any remorse when Mark, in a drunken rage, attempted to rape her.

But life chez Mitchell was little better, and before she knew it Lisa had been marginalised from her own daughter's life and was being treated, at best, as a skivvy. Finally she had had enough, took Louise and departed for Portugal to join Mel, leaving a note scrawled in lipstick on the bedroom mirror: 'SHE'S MINE'.

Phil followed her, and somehow returned triumphantly clutching Louise in November. But what of Lisa? Peggy found her passport in Phil's luggage and suspected the worst (but, of course, kept her mouth shut: this was family). Sonia was less circumspect and went straight to the police, saying that Phil had murdered Lisa. As the year drew to an end, the net was tightening around Phil, as more and more circumstantial evidence pointed to foul play in the disappearance of Lisa.

Little Mo and Trevor

We last saw Little Mo twitching over what she assumed was Trevor's corpse. When she and her sisters returned to the Fowlers' kitchen to dispose of the evidence, however, it had upped and walked. They scrubbed up the blood as best they could and hoped that the whole thing might just blow over.

Trevor, however, was not the sort to blow over. After surviving Mo's attempt to iron him to death, he returned to the Square to terrorise her yet more. Rather than going to the police and telling them that her husband had raped her, Little Mo kept quiet and looked bewildered, awaiting trial for attempted murder in April.

The trial was a sensation. Trevor gave a good impersonation of a sane, injured human being, while Little Mo went completely off the rails and decided

Little Mo pays the price for her homicidal ironing habits

to change her plea to guilty. Fortunately, she was persuaded this was a bad idea, took the stand and told the court about the hell she had lived through at the hands of her abusive spouse. The jury was unmoved, however, and Little Mo went down. The sentence that was handed out in May was harsher than anyone had feared: eight years.

This was not good enough for the Slater family, who knew that Little Mo was innocent and were determined to win the appeal. Kat managed to track down Trevor's other woman Donna, now the mother of baby Sean, and persuaded her to testify against Trevor. There was a tense moment when Trevor turned up at the Slaters' house looking for Donna – but the police caught him red-handed, and Mo got out of prison in the summer.

Of course that was not the end of her suffering. Just as she was starting to build a new life with Billy Mitchell, Trevor turned up on the scene again, pretending to be all reasonable about granting her a divorce and even dating Sam Mitchell to cover his fiendish purposes. It didn't last. In October Trevor had turned back into a foaming loon, causing havoc around the Square on Hallowe'en night. He kidnapped Mo and baby Sean in the Slater house, doused the place with petrol and prepared to go straight to hell. Fortunately, Tom was at hand to rescue Mo and Sean; when he went back inside to get Trevor, the whole place went up in flames, thus giving us the third death of major characters by fire in a single year.

After that, Billy and Mo had a well-deserved rest, and were allowed to marry on Christmas Day.

Peggy and Frank

Peggy was distraught when she received a call in January informing her that Frank – to whom she was still married, although you wouldn't have known it – was dead. Overcome with grief, or at least curiosity, she headed for Spain, where the fatal car crash had taken place. At the funeral, however, she was puzzled not only to see a tall, glamorous redhead throwing a rose on to the coffin – but also to see Frank himself attempting to make a getaway.

Several irate conversations revealed that Frank had faked his own death in order to rip off large numbers of gullible ex-pats in a property scam he was running with his latest moll, Krystle. It soon transpired, however, that Krystle had both the brains and the beauty in that relationship – not difficult, under the circumstances – and she ran rings around Frank and Peggy before absconding with the loot. Peggy managed to get Frank out of trouble, but declined his kind offer to start a new life with her.

She returned to Walford minus a husband – but plus a daughter, as she'd managed along the way to find her errant child Sam pole-dancing in a dodgy nightclub. And so Sam (who looked, somehow, different…) came home to Albert Square.

Janine's Drugs Hell

The game's up for Janine

We had long known that Janine Butcher was a bad lot, but nobody could have suspected just how low she would sink in 2002. Deprived of her only source of income when Frank signed the car lot pitch over to Peggy, Janine found herself somewhat strapped for cash – which was a nuisance, seeing as she'd just developed a full-blown cocaine habit. Before long, Janine was borrowing money left, right and centre to feed her hungry nostrils, and then, when her credit ran out, she started to sell her body to her dealer in exchange for drugs. And so *EastEnders* had its first coke-addicted prostitute – a storyline which surprised several viewers of what was, after all, a pre-watershed show.

Janine took to her new vocation with gusto. Soon she wasn't just tricking with her dealer, Lee; before long she was entertaining any number of his 'friends' in order to rustle up some funds, and then she started going with anything in trousers. Yes: even Ian Beale. Fed up with Laura's constant nagging, Ian rediscovered his taste for commercial sex, and spent the first of many disastrous nights as Janine's companion.

As the year wore on, Janine became more businesslike. She started putting cards ('Blonde Bombshell!') in local phoneboxes, and took to hanging around in a selection of loosely knotted kimonos. She attracted the attentions of an extremely troubled young man, Matt, who proposed marriage to her and then attempted suicide when he discovered she was still selling her wares.

Not content with being just a prostitute, Janine then added blackmailer to a rapidly growing CV by threatening to shop Ian to his wife. Ian, far from disliking this, found the S&M overtones of the situation irresistibly erotic, and snogged his blackmailing coke-addict-prostitute friend right in front of his own son.

Strangely, there was never any shortage of people willing to help Janine, no matter how vile she became. Her sister Claire appeared, and offered to take her back to Cheshire, but left her in the lurch when she discovered out the shocking truth. Billy found Janine slumped on the allotments with an empty bottle of vodka in her hand, and took her to hospital where she just about survived.

This was a sort of turning point for Janine. She bundled up her hooker wardrobe and burnt it at the allotments, then went round to apologise to Laura for wrecking her marriage. Had Laura known what was coming, she might have thanked Janine; instead she flung a pan of boiling milk in the poor girl's face, sending her to hospital once again.

And so Janine completely unravelled. She developed acute agoraphobia – and when Billy tried a 'tough love' approach by starving her out of the house, she took to eating dog food. Realising that this was not exactly dignified, Janine pulled herself together and attempted to win Billy, with whom she had fallen in love. The end of the year saw her making a tentative re-entry into normal life, doubtless eager to put a very embarrassing twelve months behind her.

Jamie and Sonia

Jamie and Sonia spent most of the time dithering about their relationship. They split up and got back together again so often that nobody, least of all their interim partners (she had Gus, he had Zoe, Janine and even Belinda, the occasional Slater), could figure out what was going on. When Jamie told Sonia he didn't want children yet, she flipped out and started stalking her adopted baby Chloe yet again, even going so far as to kidnap her in May, before agreeing to hand the poor child back to its mother. Not bad for a girl who had only just turned 17.

After taking their indecisions to epic heights throughout the summer, Sonia and Jamie found true love after he had yet again been beaten to a bloody pulp by Phil. But some things aren't meant to be,

Sonia finds it too difficult to give up Chloe

and no sooner had they decided to make it legal than Jamie was run down by Martin Fowler who was driving without a licence. He languished for a while in hospital, just so that he could die on Christmas Day of a ruptured liver – but not before he had slipped a ring on to Sonia's finger.

Jamie takes a tumble

Sharon and Tom

Sharon returned to Walford in April, bearing bad news: her mother, Angie, had finally succumbed to a life of acute alcoholism, and died of cirrhosis of the liver. At the funeral, she met an old schoolfriend called Tom Banks, who couldn't have been all bad because at least he used to bully Ian Beale at school by flushing his head down the toilet. Tom and Sharon started a tentative affair.

When she discovered that Tom was a) married with a child and b) dying of a brain tumour, Sharon realised that this was love, and decided to fling herself into yet another deeply damaging relationship. The abandoned wife, Sadie, started hanging around the Square and occasionally trying to chuck herself out of windows; this seemed to excite Sharon, who went into business with Tom and planned to marry him.

Before things could get too serious, Tom – who was, handily, a fireman – rescued Little Mo and baby Sean from a burning building, and died attempting to save Trevor. Sharon spent the rest of the year in a daze, avoiding the square by visiting both Tom's grieving mother in Ireland and her old friend Michelle in Florida.

Tom (Colm O'Maonlai) heroically attempts to save Trevor

Ian and Laura

Not content with jeopardising his marriage by sub-contracting his sex life to Janine, Ian ended the year by throwing his long-suffering wife Laura out on to the streets on Christmas Day when he discovered that she was carrying another man's child.

Laura had spent the whole year telling Ian that she wanted children – and so, of course, he rushed straight off and had a vasectomy without telling her. Laura cheerfully went ahead with her programme, demanding sex twice a night during her fertile periods, while Ian looked smug. That look was well and truly wiped off his face when a series of tests proved beyond all doubt that his wife was with child.

At first, Ian pretended to be delighted, and jollied Laura along with frivolous conversation about what they might call the new little Beale. Then Ian dropped his long-prepared line: 'How about naming it after its real father?'

Laura was out on the streets before you could say 'Pass the turkey'.

Also...

▶ Steve has an affair with Sam, just to annoy Phil... ▶ Natalie gives birth to a son, Jack... ▶ Dot and Jim get married on Valentine's Day... ▶ Robbie is in love with Nita... ▶ Harry dies from a heart attack and leaves Zoe a cheque for £18,000, which she disposes of... ▶ Zoe and Kat take turns at going out with Anthony, who can't decide between them... ▶ Terry leaves to join Irene... ▶ Mo runs a sex chatline as 'Miss Whiplash'... ▶ Dot reveals that she had an illegal abortion when she was 21... ▶ Derek gives Martin driving lessons (obviously not very good ones), sparking rumours of an affair... ▶ Paul is obliged to look after Precious, a witness in a gangland trial... ▶ Lynne's ex-boyfriend nearly tempts her to leave Garry... ▶ Sam nearly gets a boob-job, then has a cancer scare... ▶ Alfie Moon becomes the new manager of the Vic, by rather devious means... ▶ Steven discovers that Ian is not his real father, and leaves to join Wicksy in New Zealand...

EVERYONE TALKED ABOUT...

Little Mo on trial

There's nothing like a good trial to get the viewing figures up – especially when we, the viewers, are the only ones who know exactly what went on. The trial of Little Mo had all the ingredients of classic courtroom drama: sexism, guilt, lies and intrigue. Such was the secrecy surrounding the outcome that *EastEnders* filmed two different verdicts, keeping the press playing the 'will she/won't she go to prison?' game for the weeks leading up to the trial. But we should have known: Little Mo just had to be found gulity.

▶ Having decided at the last minute not to plead guilty, Little Mo prepares to face the music

▶ A brilliant performance in the witness box seems to have clinched the deal

▶ Kat cries with relief as she believes that her sister has got off

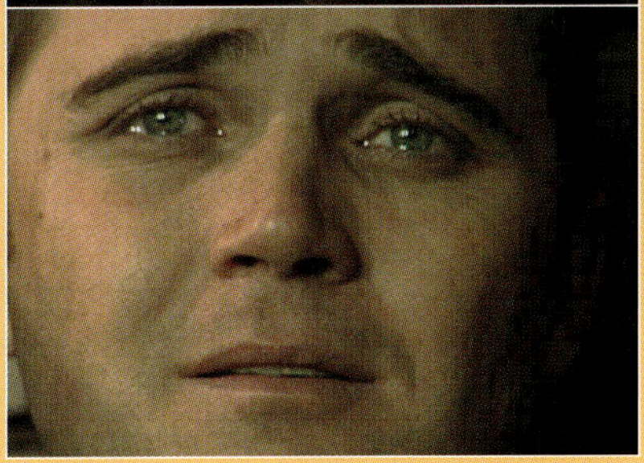

▶ But then it's Trevor's turn. He switches on the tears, the jury all go 'Aaah... ' and Little Mo goes down for eight years

Sticky Moments

***EastEnders* has always had a reputation for dwelling on...shall we say, the darker side of life? Join us on a trawl through the lower depths of Walford's most miserable memories**

Lou had a nasty outbreak of shingles in 1985, and it fell to Michelle to 'paint' the offending lesions with soothing ointment.

Arthur had the first of many funny turns when he smashed up the living room after stealing the Christmas Club money.

Colin lost the use of his legs in 1988, and became progressively ill over the coming months. At first everyone assumed it was Aids, but it turned out to be MS. Colin left to convalesce in Bristol.

Angie Watts was such a lush that, as early as 1988, she was forced to go on dialysis to repair some of the damage done to her kidneys. She would eventually die of cirrhosis of the liver.

Sue Osman was found at her son's grave wailing like a banshee and throwing earth over her head; Ali had her hospitalised (and then took to smashing things up with a crowbar himself).

Ian completely lost it when he discovered that Cindy was having an affair with Wicksy. He crashed his van, bust up his leg, then started hurling bricks and stealing guns.

Grant was prone to terrifying nightmares during his marriage to Sharon, and on one occasion in 1991 he ran amok with a sledgehammer. When he found out Sharon was on the pill, he smashed up his own pub.

Mark had several episodes of HIV-related illness after his diagnosis in 1991, but survived in reasonable health for another 13 years.

Arthur pranged his Lada in 1994, and spent several episodes modelling a neck-brace.

Hell hath no fury like a woman scorned – especially if that woman is Bianca, who responded to Ricky's infidelity by cutting up his belongings.

Meningitis has threatened the lives of both Vicki (1989) and Ben (1996), leaving him deaf in one ear.

Peggy's breast cancer led to one of *EastEnders*' most stirring storylines.

Mark was so fed up with Nick Cotton dealing drugs to his kid brother that he spiked his drink and lured him up to the top of the viaduct. Nick promptly fell off, and crippled himself.

Someone thought it would be fun to spike Sarah Hills's drink with ecstasy during a trip to Blackpool in 1996. She collapsed on the floor, then went on a trippy walkabout before being shepherded back to her hotel room.

Susan Rose's entire role in *EastEnders* consisted of being ill. Doctors eventually discovered that the source of her problems was MS.

Roy thought it would be a great idea to sort out his impotence by buying some black-market Viagra, but when he eventually managed to get chemically enhanced, Pat was having none of it.

Simon didn't handle bereavement well; after Tiffany's death, he went completely mad, kidnapped little Courtney and almost dropped her off a cliff.

Beppe took two little white pills he found in a drawer in the e20 club, thinking they were paracetamol. Foolish boy! They were, of course, Steve's amphetamines, and Beppe was rushed to hospital when he had an adverse reaction.

Only Ian Beale could have turned his daughter Lucy's suspected lymphoma into a sneaky way of getting Mel to marry him. Lucy got the all clear, but Ian kept that piece of good news to himself.

Jackie Owen's PMT made life hell for Gianni whom she regularly beat up.

Peggy joined in that popular East End sport of smashing up her own premises by wrecking the pub on Christmas Day 2001 when she found out that Harry was an incestuous paedophile.

Kat attempted suicide in 2001 and the Slater family called it appendicitis.

Zoe contracted pneumonia after living on the streets in 2001.

Janine's liver went on strike in 2002 after she had attempted suicide by drink and pills.

Derek became the Square's least likely drug baron when he took the rap for Martin's crop of home-grown up on the allotments.

Mo was up to her old tricks when she began dealing dodgy Russian fags around the Square. The fact that they fell apart when lit did little to enhance her already dubious reputation.

Thirsty Work...

Everyone in Albert Square likes a drink, but some like it more than others.

▷ Angie was permanently drunk during Den's affair with Jan ▷ Sharon decided to hit the gin in sympathy in 1985 ▷ Pete dealt with Kathy's rape ordeal by knocking back the booze ▷ Pauline coped with depression in 1989 by hitting the sherry ▷ Mark went on a prolonged bender after Gill's death ▷ Phil's drinking got a grip in 1992 and developed into full-blown alcoholism ▷ Ricky drowned his sorrows over Sam's affair ▷ Mrs Hewitt liked a little tipple ▷ Matthew became a drunken savage after Saskia's murder ▷ Janine developed a terrible thirst for vodka whilst on the game

Liar, Liar...

If you're going to tell a lie in Walford, make it a whopper.

▷ Angie: 'I've only got six months to live' (hopeless play for Den's sympathy, 1986) ▷ Donna: 'My parents have been killed in a car crash' (her mother then turned up in 1989) ▷ Nick: 'I am a born-again Christian' (he promptly poisoned Dot, 1990) ▷ Nick: 'I saw Eddie Royle being murdered by Clyde' (Nick actually did it, 1991) ▷ Beppe: 'Grant pushed Tiffany down the stairs' (Beppe knew this was untrue, 1999) ▷ Ian: 'Lucy has cancer' (she didn't, 1999) ▷ Steve: 'Matthew killed Saskia' (to avoid prison, 1999) ▷ Phil: 'Dan shot me' (it was Lisa, 2001) ▷ Frank: 'I'm dead' (he was living in Spain, 2002) ▷ Kate: 'I am not a police officer' (little did Phil know, 2003) ▷ Janine: 'I love Barry' (she pushed him off a cliff, 2004)

Burn, Baby, Burn...

Whenever an EastEnder is in a tight spot, they reach for the nearest box of matches.

▷ Den persuades Brad to torch the Dagmar in revenge for Willmott-Brown's rape of Kathy, 1988 ▷ Ali torches the café to get the insurance, 1989 ▷ Grant torches the Vic for the insurance, 1992 ▷ Frank gets Phil to torch the car lot for insurance, and a homeless man sleeping inside is killed, 1994 ▷ Barry torches the car lot again in 1995 ▷ Mel torches the e20 club, 2001 ▷ Trevor torches the Slaters' house – and dies, 2002 ▷ Billy torches Angie's Den, 2004

Ricky and Natalie prepare to leave the Square

Natalie and Ricky

Many years had passed since Ricky and Natalie's first attempt at romance, which didn't exactly end well (he gave her her marching orders, telling her she was good only for one thing). This, however, hadn't dampened Natalie's passion, and when life as Mrs Barry Evans started to get on her nerves, she realised that she had made a terrible mistake. She confided this to Ricky on one of their clandestine meetings, and he, being as easily pushed to and fro as a barn door, agreed with her. And like all secret lovers in Walford, they were very careless about who overheard their whispered endearments. Sharp-eared Pat soon waded in and handed out a few well-earned slaps.

This just seemed to sharpen Natalie's appetite, and when she saw Barry covered in remants of his dinner one fateful Pancake Day, she went off the whole idea of marriage. She persuaded Ricky to run away with her on her birthday in March, not knowing that Barry had organised a surprise party for her in the Vic.

Surprise parties in Walford always end in disaster, and this was no exception. While Barry was waiting in the pub to get the pints in, Natalie was packing Jack into the back of the car, ready to leave Walford with Ricky. Barry flung himself in front of the departing car, which could have been nasty for the car, and attempted to talk Natalie out of it. After much hysterical sobbing in the Vic toilets, Natalie decided to follow her heart. Then Janine waded in, gleefully telling Natalie that Ricky had slept with Sam – and so Natalie left on her own.

In the aftermath of this birthday party from hell, Roy discovered that Pat had known about the affair all along, and promptly dropped dead of a heart attack. Barry blamed Pat for his death, Ricky blamed Janine for everything, and we entered spring with a Square full of extremely depressed people.

Janine, Barry and Paul

After the sudden collapse of his marriage and the death of his father, all in the same week, Barry was in need of a bit of sympathy. Enter Janine, wreathed in smiles, telling him that he really needed to move on with his life and do something with all that lovely, lovely lolly that he'd inherited. Barry realised that Janine was a true friend...and, with that, his days were numbered.

For the rest of the year, Janine played Barry like a fiddle. She got a job as a manager at the car lot,

Janine crosses her fingers and says, 'I do'

and by May she'd moved in with him, and did her damnedest to cheat Pat (her own stepmother, remember) out of any inheritance from Roy. When Barry saw Janine washing down cars in a skimpy top, he began to realise that they could, perhaps, be much more than just friends. Unfortunately for him, he wasn't the only one; an equally wolfish Paul was also admiring Janine's skill with a bucket and sponge, and was quick to make his move. Janine admitted to Paul that she was taking Barry for the ride of his life – and Paul was quick to bed her and demand a slice of the action.

For a while it seemed like the perfect scam. There was only one fly in the ointment: Janine actually had to have sex with Barry. Her prostitute training came in handy there, and she barely even flinched when he proposed marriage towards the end of the year. Janine persuaded Barry to tie the knot in Scotland on New Year's Eve – and looked forward to being a merry widow, as she believed that Barry was about to drop dead from a heart murmur. Paul (Barry's best man, naturally) was waiting in the wings to console her. But, sadly for all concerned, it turned out that Barry's heart was good for another 40 years at least. This was not quite the future that Janine had in mind.

Laura and Garry

Circumstances threw Laura and Garry together at the beginning of the year, when both of them were thrown out by their respective partners as a result of Laura's surprise pregnancy. Garry went meekly in the face of Lynne's self-righteous anger; apparently her recent affairs with Jason and Beppe were nothing compared to one night of drunken lust with Mrs Beale.

There was a brief *rapprochement* when Garry and Lynne went on holiday together, but after Laura racked up the guilt factor he realised that he really ought to stand by his unborn child, and ended up accompanying Laura to hospital where she gave birth to a son, Bobby (after Bobby Moore: Garry's idea). The poor little thing was sickly at birth, and had to have a blood transfusion – during which it became clear that Garry wasn't the father after all.

Laura, who always was the sneaky type, kept this piece of information to herself, and allowed Garry's marriage to collapse once again while she appropriated him as a father and provider. Garry, meanwhile, found himself suddenly in demand as a general-purpose Walford stud, and by the end of the year he was enjoying sexual relations with Laura and Lynne and even Lynne's wig-wearing sister Belinda.

Lynne and Garry decided, after much furtive sex in the back of parked cars, that they really loved each other despite it all, and Garry looked for an opportunity to tell Laura. Eventually it was left to Ian to engineer the discovery – but even then, when faced with further proof that she was unwanted, Laura did not reveal the truth of Bobby's parentage. Could he, after all, be Ian's – despite the vasectomy?

Kate and Phil

Doubts lingered about the convenient disappearance of Lisa in 2003, and so the resourceful DI Marsden decided that the best way to get a confession out of Phil was by using a honeytrap. This turned out to be the lovely Kate, who turned up in the Square to visit Phil and pay her respects after Jamie's death. Within moments she'd got her feet under the Mitchell table and wrapped Peggy around her little finger. Phil took a little more work – but, by the time he went to visit Ben in South Africa, he had at least told her he loved her.

It wasn't until Phil's return in the spring that we learned what Kate was really up to. Phil remained in blissful ignorance, and just assumed that a beautiful, intelligent woman like Kate would naturally fall for him. The rest of us realised that there had to be an ulterior motive, as proved to be the case when Kate set off for a hot date with Phil completely wired for sound. Her police controls waited in a nearby van, stuffed to the gills with surveillance equipment, and waited for the confession.

Kate (Jill Halfpenny) moves in

Things didn't go quite as planned. Phil did indeed start blabbing – and, in a rare *EastEnders* flashback, we saw how he persuaded Lisa to hand Louise over in Portugal by blackmailing her about that little matter of a murder attempt. But Phil did not kill her; instead he left her gibbering by a cliff. Kate had heard enough, and decided that she really did truly love Phil, and ripped the wire out from her underwear, concealing it in her handbag.

Phil, however, discovered the incriminating evidence, realised that Kate was a copper and was all set to throw her out. But then Kate told him she was leaving her job, and that all she wanted in life was him. True to form, Phil reacted to this declaration by smashing a bottle and holding it to Kate's throat while police officers piled into the house. She declined to press charges, thus allowing Phil to go free – for now.

Alfie and Kat

It was obvious to everyone that Alfie and Kat were meant for each other from the very first moment they met. Obvious to everyone, that is, except Kat and Alfie, who took the entire year to realise what the rest of us had known for months.

They started out as good friends. He supported her through an unwanted pregnancy and miscarriage, and through her split-up with Dr Anthony. When she went on a well-earned holiday to Lanzarote, Alfie realised that he was really, properly in love, and admitted as much to Nana Moon – who, by this stage, was so loopy that she didn't really understand what he was on about, but made approving noises anyway. When Kat returned, they both played it cool, disastrously dating other people throughout the summer – until, one drunken night, she confessed how she really felt. It might have got further, but Alfie was obliged to go out on a long wild goose chase in search of a condom, and by the time he got back to the pub, beaten and bloody, Kat had drunk herself into a stupor.

They started dating for a while, but when Alfie discovered she had been kissing Anthony again he got huffy, and all bets were off. After much toing and froing during the summer and autumn, Alfie was all ready to propose marriage – until he discovered that he'd been pipped to the post by Andy the gangster, who was all set to marry Kat in November. Alfie disrupted the wedding by announcing to the entire congregation that he loved Kat, and got a beating from Andy's friends as a result. Kat, however, was impressed, and changed her marriage plans in favour of a Christmas wedding to Alfie.

First of all there was a small matter of Alfie's previous, never-terminated marriage to get out of the way, but the decree absolute came through in the nick of time and they tied the knot in the Vic – where else? – on Christmas Day, while artificial snow turned the Square into a winter wonderland.

Kat and Alfie's white wedding

Dennis and Den

Poor Sharon started 2003 with no men in her life; she ended the year with two, although neither of them was exactly what she was expecting. She also inherited a sister who pushed the bounds even of Sharon's obsessive family-worship, the awful Vicki, who turned up on Pauline's doorstep and was instantly palmed off on her adoptive sister.

When Vicki discovered that her father had left yet another illegitimate child in this life, she was determined to find him. The trail led to one Paula Rickman, the daughter of a friend of Den's whom he'd impregnated and swiftly dumped. Paula had just died, and so Sharon and Vicki lurked around the fringes of the funeral, hoping to get a glimpse of their mysterious brother. Just as they were giving up hope, he arrived – accompanied by two prison guards.

Some weeks later, Dennis Junior got out of prison, and turned up in Walford to take up Vicki's offer of a place to stay. Within moments of his arrival he'd had a fight with Phil, and within a couple of weeks he'd had sex with just about every available woman under the age of 40. It was just like having Den himself back in town – and Sharon started to get very hot under the collar indeed, tormenting herself with all sorts of incestuous visions, even though, of course, there was no blood kinship between her and Dennis Rickman.

Dennis and Phil got embroiled in some complicated gangster business with Jack Dalton, Den's old nemesis, which was neatly resolved when Dennis blew his brains out in July. Phil promptly grassed Dennis up to Dalton's grieving heavies, which led to yet more aggressive face-offs in offices, clubs and car parks. For almost a whole summer, *EastEnders* turned into *GoodFellas*.

Sharon was horrified when Dennis dropped the little bombshell he had been saving – her father was not actually dead at all, but alive and well and living in Spain. This led to such an almighty row that Sharon and Dennis resolved it in the traditional Walford way, by having sex.

That very evening, Sharon received a surprise visitor in Angie's Den – none other than Dennis Senior. She was so distressed by this that she fled to the lavatories to throw up, leaving Dennis and Den to do a bit of father-son bonding. Den had no idea he had a son – Paula had omitted to tell him – and so, to celebrate the fact, they framed Phil Mitchell in a warehouse robbery and got him sent to prison. And with that out of the way, Den and Dennis carried on with business as usual, seducing the willing women of Walford.

Exit Phil

Phil Mitchell's days as Albert Square's brawny bad boy were numbered. Absolutely everybody in the whole of east London had reason for wanting him dead, apart from Kate, who had given up a promising police career in order to take up the much more satisfying job of being Phil's doormat and dupe.

She took to this with such gusto that they actually got married in September, and were surprised to see an unexpected guest arriving just in time to catch the bouquet: Lisa. Grief had changed Lisa from a downtrodden drudge into a shoulder-padded ultrabitch. It had even changed her hair from brown to blonde. She lurked around the Square being chillingly friendly and reasonable for a while – but it wasn't long before she was revealed as a bloodthirsty lunatic hellbent on revenge. And, like all crazy blondes in *EastEnders*, she happened to have a hitman's number in her handbag. She could never forgive Phil for taking Louise from her in Portugal, and decided that it was in the child's best interests to have her father murdered in cold blood.

Sadly for Lisa, she couldn't afford the £35,000 price tag for an execution, and so she bought herself a gun and lured Phil to an old railway tunnel in Brickley Woods. Sharon rumbled her plan, and sent Den to 'sort it'. He talked Lisa down and led her back to the Square, where she quickly became a twitching, dead-eyed alcoholic, while Phil went away on his honeymoon, none the wiser.

But nemesis was hot on his trail. When he tried to frame Den by planting drugs in the club, he'd overstepped the mark. Den deftly involved him in a warehouse robbery, and left him to face the music. Phil was hauled off to prison, Lisa was sent on her merry way with a pocket full of stolen cash and her beloved baby in her arms – you have to worry for that child, with a mother like Lisa. Phil, naturally, escaped from prison and returned to Walford to wave a gun in Kate's face, but finally Den gave him enough money to flee, and he left town on Christmas Day in the back of Ricky's car.

Little Mo

Little Mo was having quite a good year, by her standards at least. By December she was working in the Vic, her marriage to Billy was going reasonably well, and for once her family weren't at each other's throats. Trevor was just a charred memory, and the future looked rosy. She even had some new friends, among them an attractive, flirtatious regular at the Vic, Graham.

Graham, like all out-of-towners, was quickly revealed as a psychotic menace, locking Little Mo into the pub one night and raping her. Devastated, she confided in Kate and then tried to conceal what had happened – but the truth came out, and Graham was charged. But for Little Mo, there would be further, tougher consequences to face.

Also...

▶ Martin gets six months in prison for manslaughter, and, once released, robs a shop, attempts blackmail and starts growing cannabis… ▶ Mark leaves Walford for good… ▶ Dot is attacked by a mugger and has a crisis of faith… ▶ Robbie goes to India with Nita and Anish… ▶ The Ferreiras move into number 55… ▶ Vicki becomes pregnant by Spencer, but gets an abortion… ▶ Anthony accidentally kills a patient and leaves London… ▶ Sonia blames Martin for ruining her life, and then promptly has sex with him… ▶ Vicki mysteriously loses her American accent...

EVERYONE TALKED ABOUT…

Daddy's home

We hadn't seen Den since he took an early bath in the canal (see page 38), but we always knew, somehow, that he would be back, not least because the papers had been telling us so for months. In fact, when Den finally walked into Angie's Den, the only person in the world who was surprised was Sharon. Her joy was shortlived, however, and she realised that having an affair with her adoptive father's own son might make life complicated. Not to mention the fact that she had Vicki to contend with...

▶ Guess who? Yes, Sharon, it's the father you thought had died 14 years ago

▶ 'Hello, Princess...' A brief moment of father-daughter bonding before Sharon realises the full horror of the situation

▶ Sharon beats a hasty retreat to the toilets

▶ Den contemplates further ways in which he can make life hell for his abandoned offspring

Eternal Victims

Enduring misfortune and misery more than most, and lacking the pluck of their feistier sisters, these are some of life's endless sufferers.

Mo Mitchell (Slater, Morgan)

Little Mo had the misfortune to be married to a wife-beating psychopathic rapist in the shape of Trevor. It shouldn't happen to anyone – but Mo, for reasons of her own, kept going back to him, whatever punishment he dished out. Finally it all got too much for her, and she attempted to iron him to death – but, far from liberating her, this just landed Mo in prison. She found some respite in the arms of the newly nice Billy Mitchell, but it couldn't last, and there was another rapist lurking just round the corner.

Laura Beale (Dunn)

Being Mrs Ian Beale is a dirty job, but somebody has to do it. Laura came into the household as a nanny, and left it in disgrace, branded as a slut for conceiving, she believed, Garry's child. In between, Ian treated her like a domestic appliance that would cook, clean, look after the children and occasionally, if he'd drunk enough, have sex. Dignity was never Laura's strong suit, even in death – she tripped on a child's toy.

Lisa Fowler (Shaw)

She was intelligent, beautiful and young – and so, of course, Lisa had to lie down and let men walk all over her. Destiny, for her, took the unusual shape of Phil Mitchell, a man whom she alternately lusted after and tried to kill, not once but twice. She also put up with the dogged devotion of Mark Fowler, whom she married but never loved. She returned to Walford as a bleached-blonde, gun-toting vixen – but was quickly reduced to a snivelling, suicidal wreck.

Natalie Evans (Price)

After years of being shunted aside by stronger personalities like Sam and Bianca, Natalie settled down to the kind of existence she was really suited for, as Barry Evans's drudge of a wife. But life with a buffoon was not enough for Natalie, who showed a rare flash of spirit by ditching Barry for her true love, Ricky. Of course, it didn't last, and she faced a dreary future as a single mother.

Carol Jackson

From an early age, Carol was a cork on the stormy ocean of East End sex. She sired a large brood by several different fathers, but couldn't hold on to any of them – even Alan, her loyal, slow-witted boyfriend, ran off with a singer as soon as he'd married her. Discovering that she had competition for Dan in the shape of her own daughter was too much for Carol, and she had to go.

Also:

▷ Lynne Hobbs (Slater), the permanently disappointed Slater sister
▷ Ruth Fowler, Mark's miserable wife
▷ Kate Mitchell (Morton), undercover cop turned Mitchell moll
▷ Hattie Tavernier, pregnant by Steve Elliot, the pizza man
▷ Gita Kapoor, whose sister stole her husband

Janine pushes Barry over the edge

Janine, Barry and Paul

2004 was not a good year for Barry Evans. He started off as a newlywed, delighted to have a clean bill of health from his doctor, but within hours he'd learned that his blushing bride couldn't stand him and was carrying on with the best man, Paul. A clifftop tussle sent Barry bouncing to his death; Janine engineered it for Paul and someone from the hotel to find the body, and played the grieving widow to perfection.

Back in London, however, suspicions were alerted when Janine seemed a little too keen to move on from her bereavement. Natalie started dropping broad hints that all was not well, and then fell into an affair with Paul, which annoyed Janine even more. Paul accused his vengeful ex of being a sad and lonely nutcase, and decided that he'd better go to the police and tell them that Barry didn't plunge to his death unassisted. Janine, however, put on a good show at the police station and emerged a free woman, flaunting her 'innocence' around the Square. A good old-fashioned East End slap-fight between Janine and Natalie was soon forthcoming.

Janine settled into life as Walford's resident villain, running the car lot and ruining lives – most spectacularly by shopping Laura to the DSS for benefit fraud. Laura subsequently tripped on the stairs and fell to her death – and people started to wonder if, after all, Janine was some kind of serial pusher. She wasn't, as it happened, but the mud stuck and she realised it was time to leave Walford for good, but not before telling a few home truths in the Vic. She was last seen in the company of the police, who wanted to ask her a few questions…

Sharon and Dennis

The quasi-incest between Sharon and Dennis fascinated viewers and journalists throughout 2004, generating many 'Well, they're not really related' conversations in pubs and workplaces throughout the land. The sexual tension had been obvious from the moment Dennis first lurked in the Square – and by February it was positively sizzling. After a steamy Valentine's night, the horny pair went on holiday to the Canaries together (Vicki had to pull out at the last moment) – and they returned as fully fledged lovers. This didn't go down too well with Vicki, who decided that it was really all about her, and started some spectacular attention-seeking behaviour – necking a bottle of vodka, climbing up the Arches, sleeping with Ash, that sort of thing. Undeterred, Sharon and

The family that sleeps together, keeps together: Sharon and Dennis

Dennis made their relationship public – just in time for Den's return in March.

This sparked a period of intense Freudian soul-searching as father and son confronted each other's manifold shortcomings. Den raked up Dennis's patchy past, the years in care, the sexual abuse, the lack of family life, while Dennis understandably retaliated by saying that Den hadn't exactly been a model father. After a great deal of toing and froing, Dennis decided in true *EastEnders* style that 'family' was more important than personal happiness, and concluded that he and Sharon were related after all.

This couldn't last. No sooner had Dennis started a rebound relationship with Zoe Slater than Sharon realised that, after all, he was the man for her, brother or not. This led to a period of secretive liaisons, during which the guilty siblings decided that, in fact, they couldn't live without each other, and made furtive plans to flee Walford at Christmas. The bags were packed, the taxi booked – and then came the bombshell revelation that Zoe was expecting Dennis's child. Sharon quite understandably decided to leave Walford for a while and put Dennis behind her – but can this one ever really lie down for good?

The Ferreiras

Most of the younger Ferreiras began the year stranded on a Scottish moor after crashing their van, and nearly losing Tariq in a fire. It might have been better if they had, as Tariq continued to be a thorn in the Ferreira side for the rest of the year. He confessed to Mickey that he might, after all, be half-brother to the Ferreira kids – including Kareena, who he'd been dating on and off. In this we can hardly blame him, given that brother-sister relationships were all the rage in Walford in 2004.

When Ronny was stabbed by a roving gang at the end of January, Tariq was forced to confess to the family that he might, after all, be a blood relative – and would therefore be in a position to contribute the kidney that might save Ronny's life. This caused an explosion in the Ferreira household, and in one agonising episode the children were forced to accept that their father Dan (by now permanently out of the country) was regularly unfaithful to their mother, and that Tariq was one of his by-blows. Tariq eventually decided to run the risk of donating a kidney, but when he overheard his new brothers discussing the fact that they never could stand him, he decided to take his organ and walk. After much soul-searching he went ahead with the operation, but the rest of the clan seemed far from grateful. Later in the year they had other problems to confront, when Dan's unpaid mortgage brought bailiffs raining down left, right and centre.

Little Mo

In the wake of her rape, Little Mo's world fell apart. First of all she was terrified of HIV; then she discovered she was pregnant with Graham's child. Billy couldn't bear the idea of bringing the child up as his own, and under the pressure of this decision their marriage collapsed. Little Mo did all she could to salvage things, even going so far as to contemplate terminating the pregnancy, but when she learned that her husband was an arsonist, she decided that, after all, she would leave the Square and have the baby on her own.

In her absence, Charlie had to face the music for having taken the law into his own hands and beaten Graham to a pulp. When the court case came around in February, Charlie couldn't muster sufficient repentance, and told the jury he'd be proud to do it again if he could – and was duly sent down for three months. Graham, meanwhile, was sneaking around trying to screw money out of the Slaters to drop his charges, and was finally paid off with £7500 – money that Kat was obliged to borrow from the least suitable of sources, namely Andy. This was one debt that wouldn't be so easy to pay off (see opposite).

Little Mo returned for Graham's trial in November, bringing with her an infant son, Freddie.

Billy did the right thing by testifying for his wife, thereby crushing the defence's claim that she was partly consenting in the rape, and such was Little Mo's gratitude that she tried to make a go of things with Billy again. He tried hard to accept Freddie into the family, but found that he could never forget the circumstances under which he was conceived. By the end of the year, Billy and Little Mo were drifting apart again – and Little Mo drifted straight into the open arms of her brother-in-law, Alfie Moon.

Martin and Sonia

It seemed like no time at all since Sonia was blaming Martin for ruining her entire life (not to mention killing Jamie) – but EastEnders are very forgiving people, and during 2004 Sonia realised that her feelings for Martin weren't so much hate as love. She had a bit of a makeover in time for Valentine's Day, which opened Martin's eyes – and the young couple started dating seriously. Sonia was a great support to Martin when Mark died in April, and it was this experience that made him decide just how much Sonia really meant to him. As Martin became head of the Fowler family (and we all realised just how old we must now be), he cemented the relationship by proposing to Sonia on the allotments.

There was a long period of disagreement about what sort of wedding they'd have. Pauline wanted them to have a proper Walford knees-up, whereas Sonia and Martin preferred sneaking off to Southend instead. That's where, after a lot of last-minute misgivings, they tied the knot in June, much to Pauline's chagrin. She had the last laugh, though: the newlyweds were obliged to move in with her, as they didn't have enough money to start up on their own, and so she had them under her thumb for good.

Martin found his wedding vows easy to forget, and in the autumn he accidentally had sex with Sarah, a deeply unstable waitress at Angie's Den, who started stalking him in an East-End remake of *Fatal Attraction*. Martin realised the error of his ways, confessed all to a forgiving Sonia, and got stabbed for his troubles – by Sarah, fortunately, not Sonia.

Mr and Mrs Martin Fowler start their married life away from Walford

Kat, Alfie and Andy

Never borrow money you can't pay back; you never know what trouble it will land you in. Take the case of Kat Moon, whose debt to Andy led her into the unenviable position of having to have sex with her creditor in order to prevent him from murdering her husband. Unfortunately for Kat, Andy had a video camera running at the time, and made sure that Alfie saw their little reunion, black lace lingerie and all. Alfie – who had managed to borrow the money from a loan shark without having to have sex with him – was understandably miffed, and for much of the year Mr and Mrs Moon were barely on speaking terms. Their marriage suffered accordingly, and even the near-death experience of the collapsing fairground in June wasn't enough to bring them back together for long.

Alfie's nagging jealousy drove Kat away in the autumn, and when she returned she was a broken woman. She was drinking heavily, and lost no time in lapsing back into her old ways by picking up some random bloke in the pub. Her family disowned her, and the marriage was finally over. Kat had nowhere to go but away from Walford.

The year's end found Alfie back where he started, broke, homeless and alone. The pub had been sold out from underneath him, his wife had gone, he had no money, and nearly spent Christmas

The honeymoon period is over: Kat and Alfie's marriage falls apart

on the street – but fortunately the Square rallied round, and what remained of the Moon family spent the festive period with Ian Beale.

Den, Chrissie and Kate

Den had barely got over the shock of finding that his son and adoptive daughter were having an affair, than his past turned up to haunt him in the elegant shape of Chrissie – his wife. It came as a shock to everyone, not least Den, to discover that he had a wife, but then he always was a bit vague on the matrimonial side. Chrissie was his partner in more ways than one out in Spain, and arrived in Walford demanding her share of the money from the sale of their business. Rather than taking the £40,000 that was hers, she took Den back instead, which proved that she wasn't such a great businesswoman after all. For the rest of the year she had to put up with Den's womanising ways, and

Meet the wife: Den and Chrissie (Tracy-Ann Oberman)

was horrified to discover that he was having an affair with Kate, her new business partner in the salon. Chrissie retaliated by giving Kate a revenge haircut.

Den couldn't stand the heat, and disappeared to Spain for a while; when he returned, his troublesome youngest, Vicki, was having an affair with a 46-year-old man, Tommy, and Sharon and Dennis were back in business again. His attempts to rein his daughters in resulted in them both leaving Walford, but what did Den care? He had the Vic back.

Den's purchase of the Vic stands out as one of Walford's more memorable hustles. Marcus Christie, the mild-mannered solicitor, persuaded Sam Mitchell that her brother Phil was in dire need of money, and she dutifully sold off all her assets in order to save his life. The Arches went to Ian, and the Vic went to Den. When Sam turned up to meet Phil, he wasn't there – and Marcus had scarpered with the money. The last time we saw him, he was shaking hands with Den, who was finally back at the Vic where he belonged.

Sam and Andy

Sam Mitchell has an excellent nose for a villain, and will, if possible, get emotionally involved with him. She lost no time in falling for Andy, an obvious criminal if ever there was one, and was blithely carrying on with him all the time that he was blackmailing Kat and ruining her marriage. Andy,

Andy (Michael Higgs) moves in on Sam

believing Sam to be fabulously wealthy, led her to the altar in September (Peggy came back for the wedding) – but soon found that he couldn't get his hands on the Mitchell millions, and so started mistreating her instead. When Sam was obliged to sell the pub and the Arches – and promptly lost all the money – she returned home penniless, and was pretty soon homeless as well, as her charming husband threw her out on the street. Minty, who had always carried a torch for her and tried to warn her about Andy, picked her out of the gutter and gave her a roof over her head.

Also...

▶ Zoe and Kelly contemplate an affair... ▶ Billy torches Angie's Den... ▶ Yolande and Patrick get married... ▶ Nana Moon's heart is broken by her fiancé, Wilfred... ▶ A fairground ride collapses in Albert Square and Lynne miscarries as a result of the accident. She decides to leave... ▶ Garry then discovers that he's not Bobby's father and considers suicide... ▶ Paul grasses Andy up to the police; he evades arrest and gets his revenge at Christmas... ▶ Dot falls ill... ▶ Stacey Slater, Charlie's niece-of-shame, arrives and causes havoc ... ▶ Mickey's ne'er-do-well family, the Millers, arrive in September and quickly establish themselves as criminals ... ▶ 13-year-old Demi Miller has a baby...

EVERYONE TALKED ABOUT...

Kat's adultery anguish

What's a girl to do? Ten thousand pounds in debt to a man she nearly married the previous year, with her husband getting into trouble with loan sharks, Kat had little choice but to find alternative methods of payment. And so she delivered herself up to the wicked Andy, and in one afternoon's 'work' wiped the slate clean, which places Kat among *EastEnders* top earners. Unfortunately, Alfie didn't see it that way, and by the end of the year Kat's unorthodox credit-management scheme had destroyed their marriage.

▶ The fatal undies arrive, and Kat realises that Andy really does mean 'business'

▶ In full warpaint, Kat pleads for her virtue. But it's too late! Thank goodness for waterproof mascara

▶ Timing was never Alfie's strong point, and he arrives to pay the debt moments after Kat has coughed up

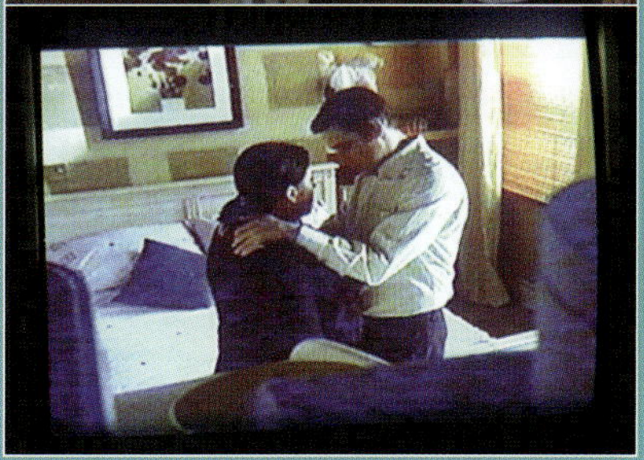

▶ Like many a wayward Walford girl before her, Kat discovers that her misdeeds have been recorded for broadcast

Poster Boys

There have always been plenty of attractive young men in *EastEnders*, whose main purpose seems to be to please the show's sizeable straight female and gay male audience.

Dennis Rickman

Since he first arrived in Albert Square one dark night in 2003, Dennis has been involved in plots involving murder, drugs, violence, you name it. But they're not fooling us: his real job description in *EastEnders* is 'lust object'. From the very first episode, he seemed unable to keep his clothes on for long, and within a couple of weeks he'd seen the inside of most of Albert Square's bedrooms. The fact that he's a jailbird and a killer gives him excellent rough-trade credentials, but now we know that he's a vulnerable, wounded little boy just searching for love, it looks like Dennis's reign as Walford's number-one pin-up is assured.

Joe Wicks

Poor young Joe was a tormented soul, the dumped offspring of David Wicks, traumatised by the loss of a sister and battling incipient schizophrenia. All of this, however, was entirely secondary to his real function in the show, which was to hang around the Square looking troubled and handsome – something he managed to do even at the height of his mental illness.

Clyde Tavernier

As a boxer, Clyde had ample opportunity for taking his shirt off – something which, like Dennis Rickman, he did at the drop of a hat. Unlike Dennis, however, his purpose was almost entirely decorative, and Clyde had very little else to do in the show, other than to dally improbably with Michelle and to do the odd bit of kidnapping.

Spencer Moon

Bright-eyed, eternally vulnerable Spencer breezed into Walford under the wing of his older, wiser brother Alfie, and quickly replaced Jamie Mitchell as the object of younger viewers' affections. He's been chewed up and spat out by half the women in the Square, but keeps coming back for more – will he never learn? Probably not: his weakness is his greatest strength.

Jamie Mitchell

With his floppy, David Beckham hair, his chiselled features and general air of vulnerability, Jamie was the ultimately bit of cockney totty for many viewers. In plot terms, he existed largely as a punch bag for older Mitchells (both Billy and Phil regularly battered him) and as a stud for the local girls, including Janine, Zoe, Nicky Di Marco and Belinda Slater. It was Sonia who got him, of course, which must have given hope to millions – but just when things were going well, he fell victim to Martin Fowler's terrible driving. And so Jamie remains forever young, forever blond, forever beautiful.

Also:

- ▷ Sanjay Kapoor, a hit with the ladies – of which he was well aware
- ▷ Matthew Rose, Steve Owen's victim and nemesis
- ▷ Troy Harvey, one for the older ladies
- ▷ Aidan Brosnan, mothered by Pauline and almost destroyed by Mandy – he should have concentrated on his footie
- ▷ Beppe Di Marco, the Italian Stallion

Mal Young was Head of Drama Series for BBC from 1997 to 2001 and Controller of Drama Series from 2001 to 2004

Going **Forward**

No drama gets to celebrate its 20th anniversary without staying true to its roots. *EastEnders* has always done that; despite all the changes in society that the show reflects, it remains true to the fundamental idea of showing families and communities undergoing the real experiences that are going on in the world around us. That's how it started out in 1985, and that's what will take it forward into the next five, ten, 15, 20 years. It will always be about a bunch of people trying to get through life's problems, whether they're personal or social, about how they relate to each other and to the wider world around them.

If you look back at old episodes of *EastEnders* on the UK Gold channel, they look very dated – and that's exactly how they should look. A soap should be like a scrapbook or a photo album of the time in which it's produced, and I always hope that today's episode looks as if it was shot that very afternoon. It's about the time in which it's made, it has an immediacy and a connection with the audience that's all about the here and now. When *EastEnders* started, the world was a very different place: there were only four television channels in the UK – just – and nobody could have predicted the digital revolution, the internet, any of those things that we now take for granted. But, despite all those changes, *EastEnders* is still the number one show on the BBC for the simple reason that it's carried on doing what it's always done, telling great stories through strong characters. In 20 years' time we'll look back on 2005 as 'the good old days of *EastEnders*', because people will always remember the past with nostalgia and fondness.

The stories that will take it through the next few years are already on page nine of your newspaper. They're the little stories about changes in the fabric of our society that affect us all on a day-to-day basis. Society has changed so much in 20 years – we're entering a much more classless phase now, like it or not, when people who would have been called working class are now indistinguishable from the middle class. They have the same aspirations and the same concerns: getting their children into good schools, for instance, or buying property. And the moral landscape is very different. There are subjects that *EastEnders* was very brave to tackle in the 80s that are now discussed in every playground in the country: divorce, broken families, drugs, rape, all the darker side of life. A big show like *EastEnders* can bring those subjects into the family arena, which is where they belong – not tucked away in a late-night documentary.

EastEnders' viewers are younger and more demanding now than they were when it started, and it's important for the programme makers to reflect that. But that doesn't mean that it's going to be chasing audiences with sensationalist storylines. Okay, every once in a while it'll have a big, fun story like 'Who Shot Phil?', but the real fabric of the show will always be the kitchen-sink stuff. It's that small-scale drama that people really get involved with. I loved it when people said to me, 'I was pregnant when Pauline was pregnant with Martin' or 'I went to college at the same time as Michelle' – it meant that the show truly reflected the lives of the people who watched it. There are kids watching it now who weren't born when the show started, and it will always provide landmarks in their lives. They say pop music is the soundtrack of our lives – well, I've always wanted *EastEnders* to be the home video.

I've spent the last 20 years working on big popular dramas that are at the heart of the schedules, and seven of them on *EastEnders*, and I've learned in that time that you can never rest on your laurels. You're only as good as last night's show. *EastEnders*' viewers love the show, but they're also very hard on it – and just because they've watched it for a long time doesn't mean they're going to stay with it if it's not giving them what they want. In a TV environment where there's so much competition, you can't assume that an audience will remain loyal. *EastEnders* has to make sure that it carries on taking its viewers on an emotional journey through the lives of characters that are, essentially, just like them. That's the deal, when you commit yourself to watching a soap: you're going to get a reflection of your life, and you're going to be taken on an emotional rollercoaster.

In the years I was at *EastEnders*, I saw a lot of changes – actors came and went, we grew from three episodes a week to four, we'd gone through enormous social change – but my touchstone for what made a good episode remained very simple. I always asked myself, 'What would Pauline think of it?' She was my barometer of everything that we did in the show. Did a storyline seem like something that could honestly touch her life? How would have she reacted to a situation or a character? As long as Pauline is in the show, I think *EastEnders* will stay in touch with its roots, and that's what will ensure its survival.

Of course there will be change; it's in the nature of any long-running show that it's in a permanent state of evolution and flux. People who were with the show for a long time, including myself, have moved on, and new people have come in. But the essence remains the same: strong, complex characters going through problems with their relationships, their work, their health and their neighbours. That's always been what *EastEnders* does best, and whatever changes may take place in the details, that's what it will carry on doing.

Mal Young

Index

Characters and Illustrations in italic

The author and BBC Books would like to thank BBC TV archives, BBC Photo Library, BBC Picture Publicity and *Radio Times* for their generous contribution of pictures to this book. We are also very grateful to all the photographers whose work is featured in this book.